A Machine Learning Approach for Cost and Effort Estimation in Agile Development Process

AF443094

Vyas Manju

TABLE OF CONTENTS

LIST OF TABLES

LIST OF FIGURES

LIST OF ABBREVIATIONS

SDEE	:	Software Development Effort Estimation
PCA	:	Principal Component Analysis
XP	:	Xtreme Programming
SVR	:	Support Vector Regression
LR	:	Linear Regression
RBF	:	Radial Basis Function
ANN	:	Artificial Neural Network
SP	:	Number of Story Points
BP	:	Backpropogation
MMRE	:	Mean Magnitude of Relative Error
ML	:	Machine Learning
ASD	:	Agile Software Development
DT	;	Decision Tree
PRED	:	Percentage Relative Error Deviation
MRE	:	Magnitude of Relative Error
MMRE	:	Mean Magnitude of Relative Error
MLP	:	Multi-Layer Perceptron

CHAPTER 1
INTRODUCTION

CHAPTER 1

INTRODUCTION

1.1   INTRODUCTION

Software project management is a key area in the field of computer science as software now-a-days impacts every area related to human life. Managing software means the process for development and the maintenance of software must be completely controlled using various pre-defined set of rules. As the software development process has to follow various parameters and a well-defined life cycle to ultimately deliver all the requirements gathered from the customers hence it has become quite time consuming and expensive process. It is also an evident fact that failure in software is caused mainly due to faulty practices used in project management. Using the right and optimised practices for software management helps both client as well as developers. Because of all the factors the need for highly reliable software is increasing. The reliability of software is mainly dependent on two factors: the selection of proper model for development and the estimation of various parameters. During the last few decades, the former area has been a research interest for many researchers resulting in development of many reliability models. Hence, currently parameter estimation is considered to be a primary activity in software reliability prediction and broadly the most important aspect of software project management. Software reliability models only become useful if they provide a correct and optimal estimation of various parameters.

A successfully completed project means that the project is developed within the planned budget and timeline which is mostly related to accurate effort and cost estimation whereas inaccurate estimation of effort and cost results in failure of a project in context of delivery time, cost and other parameters. Hence the most important parameters requiring accurate estimate in terms of software projects are effort and cost. The accuracy of the estimation of these two vital parameters depends on the correct estimation of size of the project to be developed, and the ability to convert the size estimate into man hours, duration and cost. (Abrahamsson, 2007)

Software size estimation plays a key role for calculating the effort required to successfully complete a project. In case of traditional development processes which mostly followed a linear sequential approach throughout the life cycle of the project development, the size estimation using Lines of Codes or function points followed a mathematical or algorithmic approach, but as the modern software industry has mostly shifted to agile development process because of its iterative and incremental approach as well as other various characteristics like reduced risk, increased customer satisfaction and rapid delivery, the size estimation is the key factor because of the reusability, modularity and the need of customers to accommodate changes throughout the life cycle. As the agile process model allows the dynamic changes in the user requirements during the development cycle so this is the preferred process model these days. Initially, the estimation of size, cost, time and effort was done using an expert's opinion or using historical data like Planning Poker and Case Based Reasoning. But the dependence of these techniques on the historical data and in absence of previous data and expert's opinion these techniques were not useful. (Aljahdali, 2015)

In a nutshell, it is observed from all the above mentioned factors that lot of research work is required in the field of parameter estimation of projects specifically developed using Agile methodology. This research work considers applying various techniques of Machine Learning for effort and cost estimation of the projects over a published dataset and proposes a novel approach based on the application of ensemble of various Machine Learning algorithms. The results obtained after application of the proposed approach are further compared with the available literature to assess the performance of the approach.

1.2   MOTIVATION

The motivation of the proposed work is to suggest the estimation industry a novel approach for the estimation of projects developed using agile methodology which might show some improvement in the current techniques used. The main reasons are:

i)   Unavailability of proper estimation technique for effort estimation of software projects developed using Agile framework:

The Agile development process has started gaining a lot of popularity recently in the software industry because of its preference to customer satisfaction and iterative development, so the techniques which were mostly developed in previous years **were** developed considering the waterfall or prototype development method. Also, various models of Agile are present and used in industry like Scrum, XP, lean programming etc. so it is very difficult to suggest a single appropriate technology.

ii)   Unconvincing results from expert based and algorithmic models:

As various expert based techniques were used initially for the effort estimation of agile projects like T-Shirt Sizing, Planning Poker etc. which were purely based on biased results so algorithmic models were suggested. But the algorithmic models also failed to produce optimum results for effort estimation. Hence various researchers suggested the application of ML technique for the cost and effort estimation of these projects for increasing the accuracy of estimation.

The earlier research suggested that around 75% of the projects fail or get over budgeted and exceed their deadlines because of inaccurate estimation of effort and cost. The accuracy of estimation is a major factor in the successful development of the project due to the unclear identification of user requirements, inaccurate size estimates of user stories, wrong estimation of complexity of implementation and skill-set of the team members. However, for a successful project completion which follows the deadline as well as budget the estimation must be conducted in early stages of development (Coelho, 2012)

The problem statement was identified considering all the above mentioned factors and considering the various factors contributing to the motivation of this work.

1.3   BACKGROUND OF THE BOOK

1.3.1   Introduction to Agile Methodology

The agile methodology is basically an iterative development model which targets customer satisfaction and incremental delivery of software. The agile framework focuses on customer satisfaction as customer plays the role as an active participant in the planning and software management process which leads to accommodation of changes at every phase of development cycle as suggested by the customers. This dynamic nature of agile requires development of various techniques which may be applied for software cost and effort estimation. The major advantage of agile methodology is that the risk is minimized as the delivery is done at the end of every iteration by dividing the complete requirements into small increments. A set of user requirements are identified in every iteration by having a discussion between developers and customers. (Cohn, 2005) There are various models of agile but the most used model is Scrum which calculates Effort by using story points and team velocity. In SCRUM model the meeting between the user and the developers is termed as Sprint and the requirements are called user stories which are measured in story points. One user story may comprise of single or multiple features given by the user. The team then develops the user stories in the "sprints", following the deadline and builds a working prototype to be discussed with users thus increasing the customer satisfaction which in turn reduces the overall risk as testing is performed in each iteration. Also any changes that are communicated dynamically in the requirements elicitation can be lodged in at any phase during the complete life cycle. (Panda, 2015)

In traditional development processes the team's manager determines the team member's workload capacity. He estimated the duration of certain tasks and then assigned work based on the time availability of that member. Agile process works on the concept of assigning work to a team to find the capacity of a member. In an agile model the software is delivered in small increments using various iterations and the feedback of the customer is used as an input for next iterations. Thus it was evident that a progressive approach is required in planning. The accurate estimation of effort incurred by a user story helps the developers to select which user story to develop in a Sprint so that the project's velocity is maximised (Ungan, 2014). The performance metrics which are used in existing literature of estimation approaches are Mean Magnitude of Relative Error (MMRE) and Magnitude of Relative Error (MRE). (Usman, 2014)

The Agile development Environment basically consists of three important factors, its iterative nature, its demand for increased customer satisfaction and quality assurance. All these factors are described below in detail:

i)   Sprint Planning- Iterative, Evolutionary, Incremental

The projects developed using agile framework are divided into sprints which are small increments of fewer tasks with minimal planning. Hence this framework basically does not involve any long term planning. The duration of sprint typically lasts from one to four weeks. Each sprint consists of a team which works cross-functional involving planning, requirement gathering, designing, coding, testing and other functionalities. At the end of every sprint, a demonstration of working product is shared with the stakeholders comprising of clients, and development team members. This practice results in risk minimisation and more adaptability towards changing requirements. The target of an iteration is not a product ready for release in market necessarily, rather is to have a product satisfying few requirements with minimal errors. The new and additional features quoted as new requirements are handled in further iterations.

ii)   Increased and Effective Communication among stakeholders

As customer satisfaction is one of the prime objectives of agile framework, which is ensured by having a continuous and effective communication among the client / customer and the development team. A Product owner is appointed by the client side, who is responsible for all the communication regarding requirements and their priorities and further for the approval of the changes done by the development team. The product owner is considered as an active member of the team and has to be present in all the Sprint meetings. A display board is used by the team and the client representative, which consists of all the planning and execution along with the back log of every sprint. This clearly shows the status of the project in every Sprint meeting

iii)   Quality Assurance

To assure the quality of the developed product, short meetings termed as "Stand-ups" are held which are basically feedback meetings. The output of these meetings consists of planning, successful executions and roadblocks serve as a loop of feedback for further iterations. Further, various practices like automation testing, domain driven design, code modularisation, constant integration etc. are used to improve the product quality and to enhance the agility of the project. (Abrahamsson, 2011)

(Abrahamsson, 2007) highlighted the difference between the Agile development and traditional development framework based on various factors like team formation and role, development environment, process used etc. Similarly various studies conducted for research in Agile development first emphasizes on how is agile different from other prominent traditional development framework. Table 1.1 summarizes the observations which describe the difference with respect to various features.

Table 1.1: Difference between Traditional & Agile Development Framework in Software Development

Feature	Traditional Framework	Agile Framework
Development Environment	Formal, Linear, Rule-based	Iterative, Informal, exploratory
Target	Optimization	Adaptability to changing requirements
Process	Sequential & Synchronous	Concurrent & Asynchronous
Team	Work-Centric with changing team members in various development phases of development life-cycle	People-Centric with same team members throughout the development lifecycle.
Documentation	Substantial	Minimal
Bugs handling	Too slow to handle bug fixes & provide feedback to the clients	Quick response to handling and communicating feedbacks regarding bug fixing
Adaptation to changing requirements	Accommodating changing requirements at the last stage of project development is difficult	Can easily accommodate changing requirements as they are handled in every iteration
Team Communication	Need based i.e. only when required, normally minimal	Extensive communication through regular meetings
Design phase	Minimum team members involved so less understanding of architecture	All team members works in design phase, hence can influence & understand architecture better
Overall View at beginning Stage	The overall view is very big at the start comprising of all the requirements, quality assurance guidelines, documentation etc.	The focus is only on the current sprint (iteration) comprising of fewer requirements & their fulfilment.

1.3.2   Types of Agile Methodologies

The literature available describes various types of agile methodologies but the most popular and widely accepted are Extreme Programming and Scrum. (Wen, 2012). The descriptions of the two models are described in detail as follows:

i)   Extreme Programming

XP also termed as pair programming works on the principles of accommodating and measuring incremental changes, values of increased communication, providing regular and honest feedbacks and practices pair programming. The focus is more on the people involved in the development process rather than on the tools, processes and documentation. (Abrahamsson, 2004). The Fig 1.1 shows the life cycle i.e. the process steps of XP development.

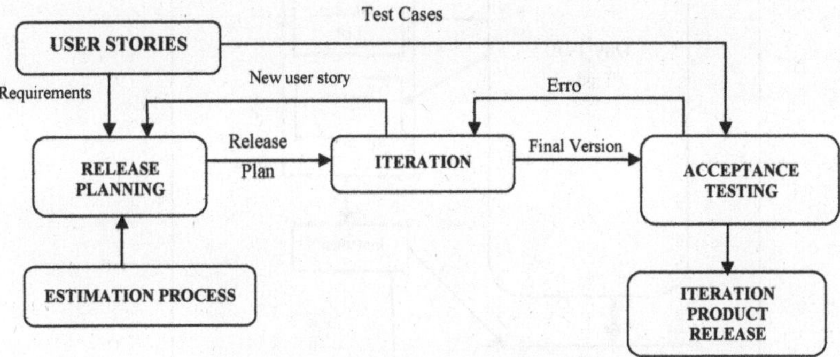

Figure 1.1: Project Development using XP

The development is done in iterations by designing every iteration through adding additional requirements, handling errors, or removing ambiguous requirements.

ii)   SCRUM

This is the most widely used and accepted agile development methodology. It works on the same principles and values along with project management as an additional practice. The project management practice involves building a backlog where all the pending requirements of a project are displayed based on their size, complexity, days required for completion, and other measures. (Cristal, 2008) Fig. 1.2 shows the development process comprising of various steps taken during an iteration (Singh, 2008)

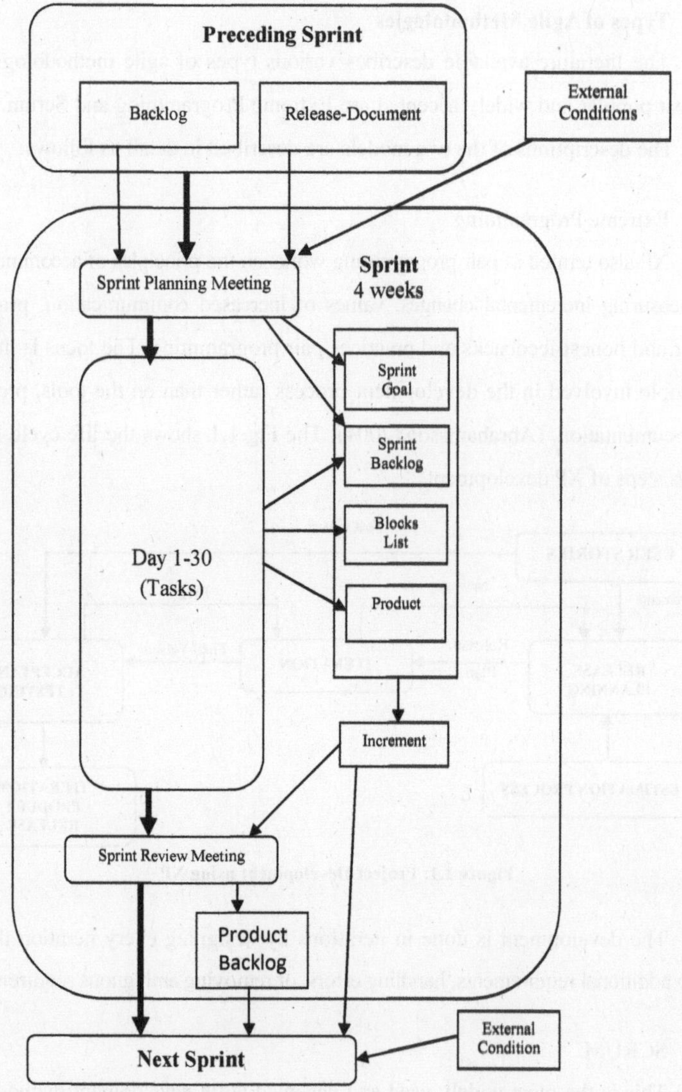

Figure 1.2: Project Development using SCRUM

Block Description of the Process as Explained by (Garg, 2016)

i) The product backlog comprises of list of all the user requirements and the issues related to them. These are created and prioritized by the customer representative (Product Owner).

8

ii)   The Sprint goal is a one line summary of the tasks of a particular Sprint. It is declared by the Product owner and has to be acceptable by the team.

iii)   Sprint Backlog comprises of the tasks to be done by the team in a particular Sprint. The list is owned and modified by the team members.

iv)   Blocks list consists of the roadblocks, pending decisions. This is created and maintained by Scrum Master.

v)   Increment is the small release of the project, which is tested and documented

vi)   Visual Feedback are the diagrammatic representations used by the team to display information like "Burn down Charts"

1.3.3   Estimation Practices Used in Agile

As per the agile manifesto, the projects with changing requirements are most suitable for agile development framework. The estimation process in agile again follows an iterative approach and is done every one to four weeks depending on the size of a Sprint. All the user requirements are estimated in terms of effort and cost which consists of man-hours required, completion time and the development cost and based on these estimates, the priority for delivering these requirements are set and are then included in various iterations depending on their business value and need.(Beck, 2001)

In traditional development frameworks, the basic requirement of estimation techniques was well formulated requirements. The estimation is done for the complete project and not on individual user requirement. Table 1.2 describes the difference in Traditional Estimation Methodologies and Agile Estimation Methodologies briefly.

Table 1.2: Comparison of Traditional & Agile Estimation Methodology

Feature	TEM	AEM
Size & Complexity	Object Points, Function Points – Calculated by using mathematical formula considering various segments like input, files, user screens etc. for computation of size	Story Points (User Stories) – Calculated by heuristic approach over user requirements as quoted by the client.
Effort	Man-month – Total time required for project development	Elapsed Time / Ideal Time – Interruption free time required for project development
Productivity	Number of Object Points or Function Points / person per month	Velocity defined as number of story points delivered per iteration

According to various systematic literature available, most popularly used techniques for effort estimation in SCRUM model are Expert Judgment, story points and Planning Poker where in various size measurement metrics are used like function points, story points etc. Also few researchers explored the use of various Machine learning algorithms to estimate effort (Satapathy, 2017). The results obtained by the application of non-algorithmic techniques like expert judgement, T-shirt Sizing or planning poker gives biased results based on various situations like the experience of the expert or the size of the team participating in the decision.

(Jørgensen, 2006) gave an observation that it is infeasible to compare available surveys for selecting one effort estimation method, as every study categorizes them differently. In their study, they categorized the techniques as: expert opinion based methods, algorithmic methods and others, consisting of other techniques. More studies have also categorized effort estimation methods to three different categories: opinion of the expert based, algorithm based models and case based methods. Further some studies have considered machine learning as the third category, (Jørgensen, 2006) in his research work gave a comparison of expert judgment techniques and formal techniques.

The most popularly used expert estimation method used for effort estimation is Planning Poker. (Usman, 2014) and Use Case Point is the algorithmic method generally used in agile methodology (Shinji, 2004). Further, the machine learning based technique for effort estimation used most widely is analogy, or case-based reasoning. (Wen *et. al.*, 2012).

Over the years various Machine Learning algorithms were proposed for effort estimation of agile projects. Few were based on the statistical methods used for analysing the historical data while few were based on Regression and Naive Bayes algorithms.

1.3.4 Categorisation of Estimation Techniques in Agile

As mentioned in previous section, the estimation techniques are broadly classified into three categories: Expert-Judgment based methods like Planning

Poker, Algorithmic models like UCP and the techniques which uses machine learning algorithms for prediction using historical data.

i)   Expert Judgment Based Technique

In these techniques, the estimate decisions are given by experts based on their knowledge and experience of the previous projects. In absence of quantified empirical data, expert estimation based methods are still applied in various situations. The major limitation of expert based methods is that these are biased by the estimator's opinion and the experience of the person does not guarantee an accurate estimate in all cases.

(Jørgensen, 2007) in his paper identified that a professional software developer who is competent enough is appointed as an expert. Despite the fact that the term expert is utilized to allude to the product proficient who does the work development and assessment, it doesn't be guaranteed to imply that the project under development is inside the skill region of the assessor. The upside of specialists assessing the work contrasted with formal techniques is that as individuals they have more data accessible and can utilize it more deftly than calculations.

There are no defined steps about how the effort is calculated in expert estimation methods as they completely depend on the unsaid information that the estimator may conceivably have. Hence, we cannot obtain similar results regarding the effort estimates (Jørgensen, 2007). A vast majority of steps of the process for expert estimation techniques are clear and thus reviewable. Though the steps used for quantifying the accuracy are not explicit. As these means of the assessment cycle depend on instinct (and inferred information), typically there is no insightful argumentation.

An expert may be a single person or a group of people may be appointed as experts. The group estimate can be converted into a single estimate with the use of various available techniques. Existing literature presented four different methods: Planning Poker, Delphi-method, unstructured group discussion and Wideband Delphi. The Delphi and Wideband Delphi doesn't have any structured process and there is no interaction between the participants. Planning Poker and unstructured group discussions involves a great deal of communication and collaboration among the participants (Moløkken-Østvold, 2007).

In a research by (Moløkken-Østvold, 2007), processes involving a group of experts were seen as useful, as they diminished biasness and over-confidence contrasted with individual expert decision. The researchers report that this is on the grounds that group conversations during the estimation uncovers extra exercises and shed light on the genuine intricacy of errands that were at that point recognized.

In Agile development framework, Planning Poker is the most widely used method for software project's effort estimation. (Britto, 2015) It is an expert judgment based technique which considers the whole development team in the decision process, then creates a single effort estimate by combining the opinion of multiple experts. (Usman, 2014)

Created by (Grenning, 2002) the Planning Poker was targeted for application in estimation and planning in software projects handled by Agile teams. During Planning Poker meeting, a client requirement is first introduced and further the story is examined, in case more clarification is required. After that, every member of the team picks an estimate from the available estimation cards. All the colleagues then, at that point, present their card simultaneously In the event that everybody chose a similar estimate that will be chosen as the authority estimate. If not individuals can examine the introduced evaluations to arrive at an agreement. After conversation, one more round is organized until all members arrive on an agreement. Assuming the requirement is considered much enormous to gauge precisely, it tends to be gotten back to the client to be parted into more modest stories. Assuming there is no agreement, the story can be deferred for later assessment. The interaction is intended to be quick yet receives significant contribution from the people who in any case wouldn't voice their viewpoints. (Grenning, 2002)

Originally, the Planning Poker pack consisted of cards consisting of values 1, 2, 3, 5, 7, 10, and infinity. These values can be deciphered as ideal programming days. These numbers are selected to show the fact that whenever there is an increase in the estimation values, there is a decrease in precision. Accordingly, the story can't be predicted accurately when the estimate in the event is more around fourteen days, which implies that a very large value must be used as the story is very large and hence the card having infinity value must be used. (Grenning, 2002)

The empirical researches studying Planning Poker application, deduced that this technique is vastly acceptable by the development teams (Haugen, 2006) (Moløkken-Østvold, 2007). Planning Poker estimation encouraged the introduction of creating subtasks like group discussions and team interactions which were otherwise forgotten. (Moløkken-Østvold, 2007) stated that the estimation by Planning Poker basically increases the accuracy and reduces the overhead which are the cases in unstructured group estimation, although there is still some gap in this area to prove these statements. These observations match with the observations given by earlier published group studies.

ii)   Algorithmic Techniques

As planning poker and other expert judgement were dependent on the opinions of the team members only and there was no fixed process or algorithm to calculate the effort, hence algorithmic models became very popular in effort estimation research. As the initial step, algorithmic models determine the size of a project. Once the size is determined, another measure which is coefficient of productivity is applied on the estimated size of the task. After all the calculations are performed as per a set of rules following an algorithm flow, the effort is estimated as output. Further, calibration is required so that they can be applicable to all the cases wherever they are used for determining accurate estimation of effort.

The algorithm models used for calculation generally uses statistical techniques, like Regression analysis. In the literature, Ordinary Least Square, which is a regression based technique is used for calibration. The OLS method works properly if the data satisfies few requirements like the size of the dataset must be large and there should be no outliers and no missing values in the dataset like extreme cases. Further, there should be no correlation amongst the target or the predictor variables and either they all should continuous or all should be discrete.

In the literature the algorithmic models, or model-based methods studied are different versions of COCOMO, Use-Case-based estimation, function point analysis methods, and SLIM.

(Satapathy, 2014) reviewed that the agile projects developed using object oriented approach predicts effort by a technique based on the use case where the size measure is Use Case point (UCP). There are two documents which are normally used in use case model, documents related to the system or the subsystem and the documents related to use cases. The system document consists of name of the system, the factors resulting in risk, use case diagram of the system, diagram showing the architecture and the descriptions of the subsystem. The document relevant to use case consists of the name of the use case, the introduction summary, context diagram, initial conditions, sequence of events, after conditions, use cases and use case diagrams for subordinate system, activity diagram, and view of incorporated classes, sequence diagrams, UI, business rules, additional requirements and other specifications. (Shinji, 2004)

The use case point depicts the size of a project. The size is measured by enumerating the number of users which are represented as actors in the use case diagram and the actions carried out by the users considering their weights in the flow of events are included. An action is defined as an event which takes place between a user and the defined system, when the transaction is either carried out in its entirety or doesn't execute at all.

Shinji, 2004 defined following steps for estimating the effort of a project based on UCP method:

Step 1 (Finding the weight of the users): In use care model, the users called as actors are divided into three categories: basic, average or advanced. A simple actor is the one who uses a pre-defined programming interface to represent another system. An average user is either a person or another system. If it is a person then it uses a text based interfaces to interact with the system and if it is system then it normally uses protocols like TCP/IP to interact with the target system. An advanced or complex actor uses a Graphical User Interface for interaction. Using this classification, the number of users in the defined software is calculated with representation of each type of above mentioned users, followed by multiplication of each number by a factor representing its weight as indicated in the Table 1.3. After that, all these values are added to get the total weight.

Table 1.3: Types of Users & their Weights

User_Category	Weight
Basic	1
Average	2
Advanced	3

Step 2 (Finding the weight of use cases): Similar to users, the use cases are also classified as basic, average or advanced. This division is dependent on the number of action carried out in a use case. The action includes both the direct and the alternative paths. For the implementation of this division, the actions or transactions must be atomic, i.e., the activities must be performed either in their entirety or not performed at all. Here the inclusion and extension based use cases gets discarded and are not taken into consideration. If the number of transactions has three or less transactions then it is called simple use case, if it has four to seven transactions then it is average, and if more than seven transactions, it is called advanced or complex use case. Based on this categorisation, a count for each type of use case is identified and then multiplication with the weighting factor as indicated in the Table 1.4 is performed. Then, all these values are added together to get the total use case weight.

Table 1.4: Types of Use Cases & their Weights

Use_Case Category	No. of Transactions	Weight
Basic	Less Than or Equal to 3	5
Average	Between 4 to 7	10
Advanced	Greater than7	15

Step 3 (Finding the value of UUCP): The addition is performed between the weight of all the actors and the weight of all use cases for calculating the unadjusted use case points (UUCP)

Step 4 (Finding the weight of Technical and Environmental factors): There are many factors, both technical and environmental which effect the effort estimation. The values assigned to these factors are used for calibration of the unadjusted use case points. The factors are shown in Tables 1.5 and 1.6 respectively. For each factor, the values are in the range of zero to five which depends upon its probable impact over the project. The zero value indicates that the factor is not relevant for the particular project and five indicates that it is essential.

Table 1.5: Factors Contributing to Technical Impact

Factor	Detail	Corresponding Weight
T-1	Easy Usage	0.5
T-2	Easy Installation	0.5
T-3	Concurrency	1
T-4	Adaptable to changes	1
T-5	Re-usable code	1
T-6	Application objectives for throughput performance	1
T-7	Online Efficient for client	1
T-8	Complexity in processing	1
T-9	Exclusive Features for Security	1
T-10	Third Party can assess directly	1
T-11	Special Training Requirements	1
T-12	Portability	2
T-13	Non Centralized system(Distributed)	2

Table 1.6: Factors Contributing to Environmental Impact

Factor	Detail	Corresponding Weight
E-1	Complex programming language	-1
E-2	Includes more workers who are part-time	-1
E-3	Skills of Analyst	0.5
E-4	Application handling experience	0.5
E-5	Motivated Team	1
E-6	Experience in developing software using object oriented approach	1
E-7	Unified Modelling Technique familiarity	1.5
E-8	Non Changing Requirements	2

The value of technical factor, is determined by first multiplying the weights of all the factors that contributes to technical impact on the project with their corresponding values and then summation of all these values to get TFactor After calculating TFactor, the value of Technical Complexity Factor is determined using the following equation:

$$TCF = 0.6 + (0.01 \times TFactor) \qquad\qquad 1.1$$

The value of environmental factor (EF) is determined by first multiplying the weights of all factor that contributes to environmental impact on the project with their corresponding values and then summation of all these values to get the Efactor. After calculating EFactor, the value of Environmental Complexity Factor is determined using the following equation:

$$EF = 1.4 + (-0.03 \times EFactor) \qquad\qquad 1.2$$

Step 5 (Calculation of UCP): For determining the value of the adjusted use case points (UCP), following equation is used:

$$UCP = UUCP \times TCF \times EF \qquad\qquad 1.3$$

Step 6 (Estimation of Effort): For estimating the total effort, the value of UCP is multiplied with a specific value (man-hours). (Shinji K. and Schigeo H, 2004) suggested a factor of 20 man-hours per UCP for a project.

iii)   Machine Learning Based Techniques

In recent years, there is an increase in research interest regarding the usage popularity of Machine learning methods in software development effort estimation. In spite of the increase in interest in this research area, researchers have still not acquired solid traction in this business yet. Since, the models based on Machine learning techniques are data-driven, so it requires historical data about the project for the model to be built. This limitation of having such historical data and that too of relevance and good quality makes it crucial to construct and implement a machine learning based model for effort estimation. Further the validation of the model's accuracy is also a crucial element. (Wen, 2012)

In a systematic literature review, (Wen, 2012) deduced that according to the existing literature, eight machine learning techniques are mostly used in software development effort estimation. To mention a few are analogy or case-based reasoning, ANN, Decision trees, Bayesian networks, SVR, genetic algorithms etc., amongst which the analogy, ANN, and decision trees were used by most of the researchers. The machine learning techniques were used to build a model by either applying as a single technique or in ensemble with others. Many of such combinations were suggested by researchers like genetic algorithms along with fuzzy logic. In many studies, first the pre-processing of the input variables is done by using fuzzy logic and then other machine learning techniques are applied.

Although lot of research has been done in the application of machine learning methods for effort estimation, but still the empirical validation has not been done, so there exists a lot of research scope in the area of applying machine learning techniques for effort estimation.

Further, it has been observed that no single technique can be termed as best suited for effort estimation. Various estimation models based on different machine learning algorithms gives accurate results in different cases. Hence, for selecting a suitable method, first the factors and contexts must be analysed and then various methods may be selected depending on these.

(Li, 2009) observed that analogy based technique used for effort estimation is basically a type of case-based reasoning. During the development of a project, features and activities of past projects are abstracted and are treated as cases. Features may consists of the no. of interfaces, methodology applied for development and the no. of functional requirements. All these cases of successful projects are stored to create a case repository. Then the effort estimation of the current project is done by extracting the most matched previous cases.

For defining the process of creating cases, first the nature of the project is analyzed and then accordingly the data and features of the cases are collected. The data is collected depending on certain rules and agreements defined by an organisation regarding the data collection. The agreement of all the team members regarding the effort estimation is mandatory else the system may collapse. The major requirement of this method is availability of a large size of repository containing the cases. Having large number of cases always gives accurate results. The collection of data must be done continuously so that a good repository of cases is built over a period of time.

Matching the current scenario with the stored cases can be done by using various approaches. Some of the suggested approaches in the literature are selection based on similar objectives, selection based on specific feature matching, selection based on recent matching and Nearest Neighbour Algorithms, The significance and importance of the features present in the cases must be incorporated in the algorithm by learning.

There are four components of analogy based model: a dataset having data of historical projects, a similarity function, a solution function and the corresponding rules for retrieval of similar cases. (Hameed, 2022) The Analogy based model follows four steps:

1. Collection of the features about the similar historical projects and creating the dataset.
2. Selection of relevant information about current project like function points (FP), lines of (LOC) and story points. This information is same as the features which were collected for previous projects.
3. Estimating the matches between current project and the previous projects. Based on these estimates, the most matched previous project's data.is retrieved. The similarity functions mostly used are weighted Euclidean distance function and the weighted Manhattan distance function.
4. Predicting metric of the current project out of the selected analogues by using the solution function. The solution function mostly used is the un-weighted average

The similarity and solution function used are described as below:

i)   Similarity function

The similarity function measurer the similarity level amongst the projects. Most frequently used similarity functions are based on Euclidean similarity (ES) or Manhattan similarity (MS)).

The Euclidean similarity function calculates the Euclidean distance between two projects:

$$Sim(p, p') = \left[\sqrt{\sum_{i=1}^{n} w_i Dis(f_i, f_i) + \delta} \right] \quad \delta = 0.0001$$

1.4

$$Dis(f_i, f_i') = \begin{cases} (f_i, f_i')^2, & \text{if } f_i \text{ and } f_i' \text{ are numeric or ordinal} \\ 1 & \text{if } f_i \text{ and } f_i' \text{ are nominal and } f_i = f_i' \\ 0 & \text{if } f_i \text{ and } f_i' \text{ are nominal and } f_i \neq f_i' \end{cases}$$

ii)   Solution functions

Once the K most similar projects are selected, the final prediction for the new project is done. It is determined by computing certain statistic based on the selected projects. The solution functions used are: the closet analogy (most similar project), the mean of most similar projects, the median of most similar projects and the inverse distance weighted mean. The mean is the average of the metric of K most similar projects, where K > 1. It is a classical measure of central tendency and treats all most similar projects as being equally influential on the cost estimates. The median is the median of the costs of K most similar projects, where K > 2. It is another measure of central tendency and a more robust statistic when the number of most similar projects increases. The inverse distance weighted mean allows more similar to have more influence than less similar ones. (Hameed, 2022)

1.3.5 Agile Estimation Metrics

This section, discusses the estimation metrics used in agile framework. Generally three metrics are used for estimating the size of agile projects: story point, Ideal day and velocity. (Kupiainen, 2015)

i)   Estimation by story point

In many cases, during the usage of agile development framework for software development, the iteration begins with incompletely specified requirements. As the iteration progresses, the details related to the user requirements are discovered. In Agile framework, a project is divided into several iterations. The results of all these iterations in terms of completed stories are combined to calculate the final result. In Scrum methodology, a Sprint is defined as an incremental section.

In Scrum, the length of iteration is of fixed duration (typically 4 weeks or 30 days) and shall not be extended. The members of the agile team measures the size of a user requirement by a unit called Story Point. The user requirements are termed as user stories and the user stories comprises of adequate information which enables the team to estimate its completion time. And the effort required for successful completion in estimated time. An index card is used to write a user story. One or two statements written in the customer's language are used to represent it. The user story cannot be defined by any predefined rule or formula. The estimation of a story point is either done by selecting a simplest story as per the opinion of the team and giving it a value of 1. Then the other remaining stories are estimated relative to it. Another approach used is by selecting a medium-sized story and giving it a number in the middle of the range of the values expected by the team and then estimating the remaining stories relative to it.

The estimation of the total completion time of each story is done by the development team. These estimates are then used by the customers to prioritize the stories in various iterations. (Santana, 2011)

ii)   Estimation by ideal day

(Osman, 2016) found that Ideal Day is another metric used for the size estimation of the software developed using agile. The ideal day is defined as the duration required for a task completion, after eliminating all other peripheral activities. Another measure defined is Elapsed time which includes all the peripheral activities as well which happens during the task completion. The peripheral activities are basically defined by the activities which are not directly related to a task like time spent in answering a query mail or time spent in as call to a client for providing support. The accuracy of estimate by ideal day is more accurate as compared to elapsed time as estimation in the number of ideal days required for the development, testing and acceptance, does not include the overhead of environment of the working team. For estimation using ideal day, and aggregate estimate is assigned to each user story. The difference between the Story point estimation and Ideal day estimation is that the former is mostly faster than the later. Also, the concept of story points is easily understood by the team members while the concept of Ideal days is more easier to explain to the members who are not active participants of the team.

iii)   Estimation by Velocity

Velocity is defined as the number of stories completed by a team in a given Sprint. The values of velocity are mostly represented by a range, like 10 to 15 story points per iteration. As the velocity is connected with the team's capacity and not with an individual's capacity, so exact velocity of the team cannot be depicted unless the same team has already worked on the same kind of project previously. Velocity is used to plan the partial product releases during every iteration,

Predicting the velocity measure requires taking a sprints comprising of several stories and dividing them into subtasks. The completion time of every subtask is estimated by considering the design time, the development time, time for testing, and other activities. Then the capacity of the team is estimated for a given sprint.

Consider a case if there are total 4 team members working for two weeks for 40hrs every week, then the total time of the team is 320 hours. Generally the base value considered for velocity is 70, so if we multiply the team's time by its velocity the total time is 224 hours (70/100*320). This means that all the sub tasks will be completed in 224 hours. Considering all the completed subtasks, by adding the story points of every subtask, suppose the velocity value is 36, thus the minimum and maximum range of the velocity is 29 to 43 story points by applying 20% on both the sides.

1.4   OBJECTIVE WISE PERFORMANCE

The first objective of the work deals with the analysis of the existing cost and effort estimation techniques used in the agile development framework. An extensive literature survey was conducted to study the various techniques. This objective has been divided into three sub-objectives: survey of basic estimation techniques, the estimation techniques used in agile development process and the machine learning based estimation techniques. A summary of observations based on these studies was formed. Further a comparison is done on the basis of the advantages and disadvantages of the various techniques and also on the basis of the accuracy metrics used for evaluation of these techniques.

The second objective of the study deals with the analysis of the various datasets used by the various researchers in the study and proposal of the existing cost and effort estimation techniques used in agile development process. An extensive literature survey was conducted to study the various techniques and the dataset used for testing the accuracy of these techniques. The domain of the used data set was found to be either academic or industrial and the type was either within-company or cross-company. Several researches have been done on the concern of applicability of the popular estimation techniques in agile development process. Story point is the widely used size metric for the projects developed using agile methodology. Various machine learning techniques can be used to improve the effort estimation accuracy. As the characteristics of the dataset used for experimental analysis affect the validation of the estimation techniques proposed, hence after doing an extensive literature survey a dataset having various factors impacting the cost and effort estimation of 21 agile projects was considered for this study.

The third objective deals with the study of various machine learning techniques used by the various researchers in the cost and effort estimation techniques used in agile development process. An extensive literature survey was conducted to study the various machine learning techniques and the actualization of these techniques for effort estimation of software developed using agile methodology. Using various observations and experimental evaluations, an ensemble technique was proposed and the results were observed to accomplish this objective.

The fourth objective deals with the implementation of the proposed approach and testing the model on dataset. The dataset used is the published dataset containing 21 rows and 8 columns, which was reduced to 3 column using feature extraction. The dataset having number of story points representing the size, team velocity representing the team's performance in similar projects and actual effort i.e. the completion time of the project in man-hours. The application of any test on data requires the data to be in the normal from so various statistical measures need to be calculated and the relationships must be plotted to check the normalisation of data. The different models which perform the effort estimation assume that the project velocity is already available. The project velocity of a project is actually calculated by analysing the velocity of same team which successfully completed the same kind of or comparable projects. If the velocity value is not known then it is very difficult to compute it. After applying the proposed approach on the identified dataset, the results were generated and further compared with the results quoted in existing literature.

The fifth objective deals with the measurement of accuracy of estimation using performance evaluation metrics. The evaluation metrices used are MMRE, MRE and MAE to study the performance of the proposed technique.

1.5   THESIS OUTLINE

Chapter 1 introduces the need for Estimation, the difference between traditional and Agile methodology and the estimation practices used in agile methodology. The categorisation of estimation practices id discussed in detail along with one technique from every category. The estimation metrics used in the agile are also discussed.

Chapter 2 introduces the review of existing studies that discusses and proposes techniques for the estimation practices used in traditional and agile development methodologies. The review is divided into three sections, the first summarizes the studies regarding estimation approaches used in traditional framework using FP and LOC based size metric. The second section considers the researches carried out using expert opinion techniques and algorithmic techniques in agile framework and the third section covers the studies using ML based techniques used for estimation of agile projects. Further, a summary of comparison is provided discussing the findings and observation.

Chapter 3 introduces the background techniques used in the proposed methodology and their working principles.

Chapter 4 introduces the methodology used for the proposed approach for effort and cost estimation of agile projects

24

Chapter 5 discusses the estimation metrics and performance measures of the algorithm. The simulation results are described in this section. The results obtained by the proposed algorithm are further compared with the existing published literature and the observations are made.

Chapter 6 gives the conclusion of the thesis and the scope for future work.

CHAPTER 2
REVIEW OF LITERATURE

This chapter describes the research work conducted in the effort estimation of non-agile and agile projects in the previous years, which consists of different techniques and approaches. The review of literature is divided into three sections, first section discusses the studies related to effort estimation of software projects developed using traditional framework, necessarily using Function Points or Lines of Code for size measurement. The second section indicates all the studies which proposes methodologies and publishes results for the estimation of projects developed using agile framework and as per the recent trend in software industry, the third section covers a study of all those researches which have analysed the use of various machine learning based techniques for estimation of software projects.

A comparative analysis is done based on the studied literature in terms of various factors like techniques used, estimation accuracy, and their applicability in various scenarios as part of summary of the chapter.

2.1   EFFORT ESTIMATION OF SOFTWARE PROJECTS

(Jogersen, *et al.*, 2006) published a systematic literature review which opened new scope for improvement in the research area of software estimation. The paper identified 304 papers related to estimation of effort and cost of software projects published in various journals and classified them according to research area, estimation approach, and context of study and used data set. Through this study the paper provided recommendations for future research which are to conduct more research on the estimation techniques like checking the accuracy of estimation techniques and use of appropriate data sets for experimentally evaluation of particular estimation techniques

(Satapathy *et al.*, 2014) applied SGB technique for effort estimation of projects developed using object oriented approach. The proposed technique used class point measure for calculating the effort as the traditional size measures like FP and LOC as used in procedural programming are not suitable for measuring the size of object oriented projects as it combines the data and procedure while procedural framework splits them. SGB works on the optimisation of results of the models which are built using decision trees. A dataset of 40 projects were used for experimental evaluation. The results obtained were then optimised which improved the prediction accuracy. The paper also compared the accuracy of the suggested approach with MLP and Radial Basis Function Network to show the improvement in accuracy using MMRE, NRMSE and Prediction Accuracy metrics.

(Aljahdali, *et al.*, 2015) proposed several models for estimation of effort for projects where Function Point and KLOC are used as size metric. The models were built using Linear Regression, SVM and ANN techniques. The various suggested models used several inputs like Lines of Codes, development methodology, Input Output files, and user inquiries for computing the effort required for development of the project. The optimal hyperplane separating the various classes of data is fund using SVM. A Multilayer FeedForward neural network with Backpropogation is used to train the model. The block diagram shown in fig. 2.1 indicates the effort and function point based models as proposed.

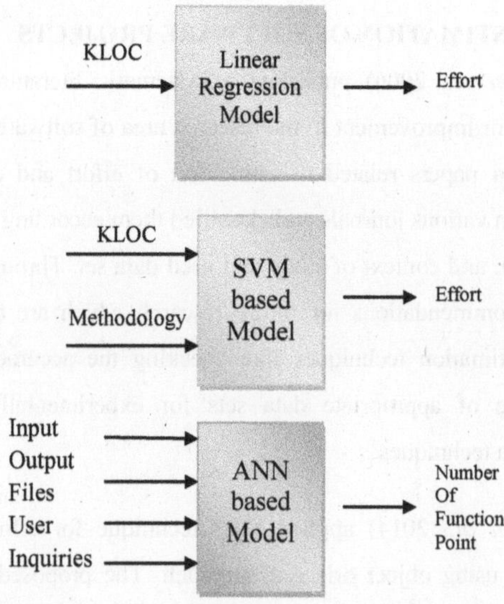

Figure 2.1: Various Models Proposed for Effort Estimation

The work concluded with the observations that effort estimation models using ANN gave more promising results in terms of prediction accuracy.

(Moeyersoms *et al.*, 2015) proposes predictive models for both software fault prediction and software project's effort prediction based on various data mining techniques. They proposed a rule extraction algorithm ALPA based on Random Forest and Support Vector Machines for regression and tested the proposed methodology on published datasets. The work proposed a predictive data mining technique based on Regression for effort prediction as the target variable in this case is continuous. Similarly another model was proposed for fault prediction based on classification which is again a data mining predictive technique for the discrete target variable. Further, association rule mining which is a data mining descriptive technique is used. The paper analysed the available literature and summarized the techniques used in software fault prediction in recent years. The analysis concluded that models based on the concept of comprehensibility performed better as compared to others. Based on this analysis they proposed the rule based models for the inclusion of comprehensibility which simply means considering the size and type of output to test how fit the classifier is. As a second module of the work, related to effort estimation again a comparative summarization was given by the researchers regarding the techniques used and the top performers in the cases. In the experimental set of proposed work, random forest based technique along with C4.5 was used for fault prediction and was tested over various datasets. Similarly, a SVR-RBF technique along with e regression tree learner was used for effort prediction of software projects. Finally, a rule extraction technique ALPA is used for comprehensibility. Lastly the prediction accuracy of both the models was tested using RMSE and Recall. The results showed that the proposed model gave better accuracy as well as comprehension as compared to previous work.

2.2   EFFORT ESTIMATION OF AGILE PROJECTS

(Abrahamsson *et al.*, 2011) suggested a technique for predicting effort using user stories. The work proposed the applicability of this technique for Agile software projects where requirements may change throughout the development life cycle. They applied the method to two industrial datasets consisting of agile software projects of different structure and size and showed that effort estimation gives accurate results if user stories are drafted in structured format. The study identified that the challenges faced for estimating projects developed using agile methods are more as the requirements may be specified at any point of time. To work towards these challenges the paper proposed a novel method for effort prediction where predictors extract data from user stories automatically. The following model as shown in Fig. 2.2 was proposed which as a first step defines some predictors like number of characters, the priority of a user story and presence of few defined keywords for automatically extracting user stories and further, the effort is estimated.

Model Construction

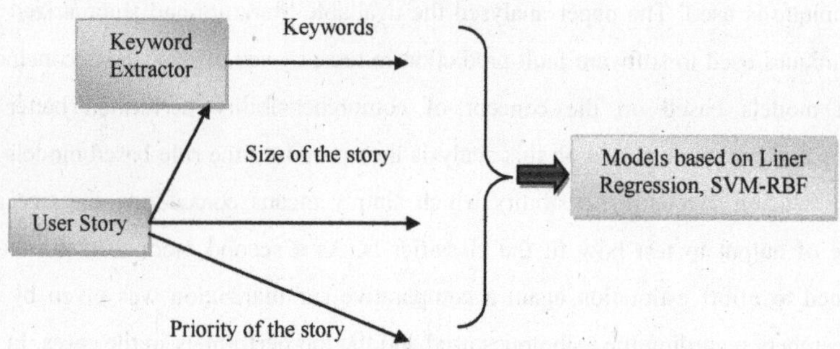

Figure 2.2: Data Extraction Model for Effort Prediction

The model was tested over two case studies, by analysing the descriptive statistics of the datasets and the prediction errors were compared with the previously published works.

(Power, 2011) proposed a new technique called Silent Grouping to complement the Planning Poker technique used for estimation of agile projects. The work studied that there are several challenges faced during application of planning poker technique for sizing user stories. The paper used a dataset of Cisco's Unified Communication Business Unit, containing the experiences of seven teams working on Scrum framework. Further, the paper indicated the applicability of the proposed technique in distributed and co-located teams.

(Coelhlo *et al.*, 2012) proposed a story point method for effort prediction in agile and highlighted the scope for future research considerations. They used the following block diagram as shown in Fig 2.3 for depicting the steps of effort calculation using story point approach.

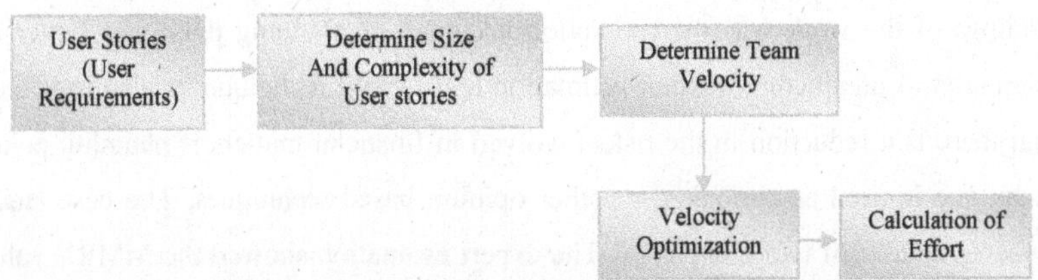

Figure 2.3: Story Point Approach for Effort Estimation

(Usman *et al.*, 2014) provided a detailed discussion in the area of estimation of projects developed using agile. They conducted a SLR in which total 25 studies were included for analysis. The major findings were the techniques used for estimation, the metrics used for size measurement, the metrics used for measuring the accuracy of prediction and the cost drivers which are most frequently in ASD. The results of SLR was published based on few research questions. The first research question framed was regarding the estimation techniques used in agile. It was studies that the expert judgment and UCP method and its modified version were the most popular amongst other techniques. The accuracy metrics used by these techniques were also listed and it was found that MMRE, PRED and MAE are the most frequently used evaluation metrics by these techniques to check the accuracy of prediction. The values of the accuracy metrics achieved by the techniques were also shown and compared. The size metric used was no of story points mostly, with few indicating use case points for object oriented projects. Another research question targeted the use of cost drivers and it was shown various factors which influences the cost of a project like skills and experience of development team, the size of the task, the test risk factor, test efficiency factor and many more are considered by the relevant published researches. The characteristics of the dataset used by all the studies were also evaluated and it was found that most of the studies used a secondary dataset based on industrial context, but it was further observed that the limited size and absence of cross-company dataset available for research poses a research gap in the area.

(Gandomani *et al.*, 2014) provided a comparison between the planning poker technique and the Wideband Delphi technique with the help of two case studies. The findings of the work was the estimation accuracy of planning poke was better as compared to unstructured expert estimation and Delphi technique. It also indicated that there is a reduction in the risks involved in financial matters if planning poker technique is used as compared to other opinion based techniques. The case study selected dataset of two companies. The expert estimation showed the MMRE value of 14.8%, Delphi method gave MMRE of 7.6% and Planning Poker gave minimum error value of 7.1%.

(Hamouda, 2014) considered projects of CMMI level 3 and proposed a technique for measurement of the size of the software using story points in relative terms for these projects. The paper first talks about the applicability and challenges of adoption of agile in CMMI organizations. The complexity of a particular user story is dependent on the skill set of the team handling the project, hence one project team may consider it as a complexity level 1 and another as level 5. This difference results in difficulty in the adoption of agile in CMMI as the sizes must be relative. In this paper a new methodology having variation in the traditional approach of sizing a story point is proposed so that it can be applied in CMMI organization. The methodology basically works on estimating the requirement sizes by defining and using a reference library of requirements and by considering all the factors, both technical and environmental affecting the project size. Further, a concept was introduced and was defined as productivity factor so that all projects may be uniformly scaled. The productivity factor normally is obtained by calculating the average of velocities of all teams. Further, a multilayer neural network model as shown in Fig 2.4 was used in the proposed methodology. Following model was used for prediction.

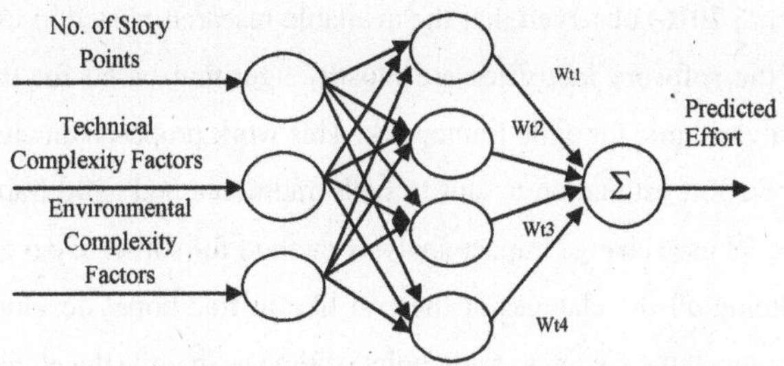

Figure 2.4: Model Proposed by (Hamouda, 2014)

(Ungan *et al.*, 2014) compared the use of two measures used for the measurement of software projects. One is number of story point and another is COSMIC functional points. It was indicated that COSMIC is a functional size measurement method used in academics and industry. The size is measured in standard functionality level known as Functionality Process and then is further divided into Data manipulations and movements like read, write, Entry and Exit. By the use of case study the effort estimation accuracy of the two models, one using no of story points and another using cosmic points was compared. The COSMIC points were calculated by the researchers and the number of story points used by the case study of a software industry were collected. Regression and ANN based techniques were used to build the model for cosmic function points and then accuracy of estimation was measured using MMRE and PRED. The results indicated that the model using multiple regression method and developed using cosmic functional points as the predictor variable gave highly accurate and applicable results, while the model developed using power regression and polynomial regression taking as input no of story points were less accurate.

(Tanveer *et al.*, 2016) used a dataset of Germany based multinational software industry and conducted a case study research. The company used Agile development framework The results indicated that the estimation accuracy is affected by several factors including the experience of the development team and their skills. The study concluded that there must be a tool or a rubric for evaluating experience and skills of the team which also considers the various cost drivers for improving the accuracy of effort estimation process.

(Basri *et al.*, 2016) observed that the available research related to estimation models used in the software industries are mostly algorithm based for traditional framework non algorithmic for agile framework. This work proposed an algorithmic change model for effort estimation to suit to both traditional and agile frameworks. The proposed model uses change impact analysis method for software development. Rather than handling all the changes at the end like in traditional development or trying to incorporate all the changes at any point of time as in agile development, the proposed model first estimates the amount of effort and time that would be required to implement a particular change. The model is then evaluated using a case study of six traditional and 6 agile based software projects. The results of the experiment shows the validity of its applicability to both the frameworks. The evaluation metrics used were MMRE, Pred(25) and MdMRE and the results indicated better performance for the proposed model.

(Sehra, *et al.*, 2017) in their systematic literature review identified and represented various research patterns in the field of Software Effort Estimation by analysing 1178 related articles. The study targeted at helping the researchers identify the potential research areas by semantically mapping the research trends to analysed research core areas.

2.3 MACHINE LEARNING TECHNIQUES FOR ESTIMATION

(Wen *et al.*, 2012) published a SLR consisting of empirical studies on various models of machine learning published in 1991-2010. The paper analysed four key areas which are: Machine Learning technique used, estimation accuracy, analysis of various models and estimation context. Around 80 primary studies were explored and concluded that total eight Machine Learning techniques are generally applied in Software effort estimation and proved that the models based on Soft Computing gives better predication accuracy as compared to non ML models. Further, it mentioned that the accuracy of estimation varies when same ML model is applied over different datasets or different experimental designs. The SLR was conducted by developing a review protocol which included six stages: defining research questions, designing a strategy for searching, selecting the appropriate and relevant studies, assessing the quality of publications, data extractions and data synthesis. The following fig. 2.5 outlines these stages.

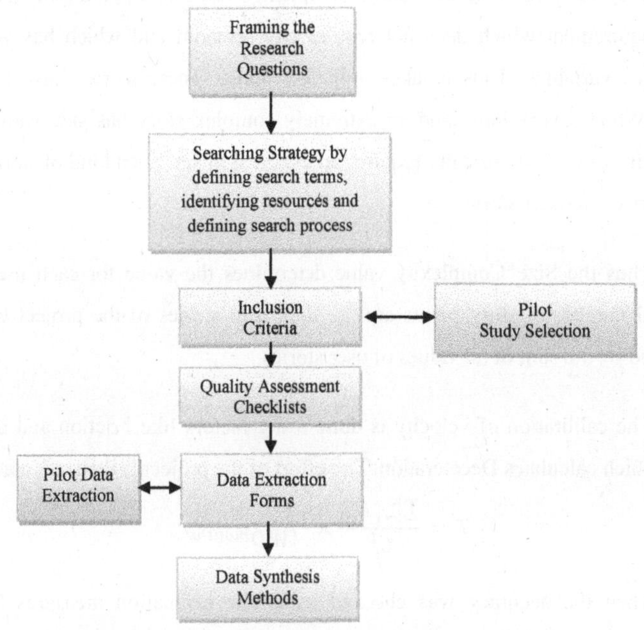

Figure 2.5: Stages of Conducting Systematic Literature Review

The review concluded that very less research has been done on the applications of Bayesian Network, SVR, Genetic Algorithms in the domain of software development effort estimation, hence these areas can be explored by the researchers. Further, it mentioned that the data sets available in this domain are very small in size, hence it suggested that researchers must share their proprietary datasets after removing the confidential information.

(Ziauddin *et al.*, 2012) developed a mathematical model which is used to predict effort. The model was calibrated on a 21 row dataset corresponding to 21 projects. The columns are no. of user stories indicating the size and the team velocity indicating the team's capacity that is the number of user stories completed by the team in a sprint or in one unit time. The user story is a user requirement, which is measured in a unit called story point. There are two features for the representation of a user story: one is its size and second is its complexity. The values of size and complexity varies from 1 to 5. A very small and least complex story is indicated by the size value of 1 and a complexity value of 1. This type of story is direct requirement which does not require any research and which has very less number of variables. Thus it takes only few hours. These stories have localized effects. While a very large and an extremely complex story has size value 5 and complexity value 5. It basically requires an expert skill set. Such kind of stories have great impact on other stories.

Thus the Size*Complexity value determines the value for each user story. The total number of story points are the total user stories of the project which is calculated by the sum of all values of user stories

The calibration of velocity is done using factors like Friction and dynamic forces which calculates Deceleration. The effort of the project is then calculated

$$T = \frac{\sum_{i-1}^{n} ES_i}{C_i^D} \times {}^1/_{WD^{months}} \qquad 2.1$$

Then the accuracy was checked using the evaluation measures MMRE, PRED. The MMRE observed was 7.19% and Prediction accuracy observed was 57.14%.

(Nassif *et al.*, 2013) proposed a model which applied machine learning techniques fuzzy logic and neural network over the use case point algorithmic model for the projects developed using object oriented approach for better estimation results. Use case diagrams were used as input to the model based on logarithmic transformation of linear regression model for calculating effort. The effort is considered to be dependent on the size and team productivity. The productivity factor was predicted using the equation for multiple linear regression and adjusted using the fuzzy approach. Further, a multi-layer perceptron model was also proposed using k-fold cross validation and the results of both the models were compared and analysed. The results indicated that the model based on log linear regression gave better results for smaller projects while the one based on MLP gave better results for the projects requiring large effort. The evaluation metrics used for checking the prediction accuracy were MMRE, RMSE and MAE. As the selection of technique used for regression is based on the relationship between the dependent and independent variables, hence the analysis was done for the relationship between size and effort of the software projects. Although few previous works indicated a linear relationship between size and effort but in this work it was verified that the relationship is mostly non-linear. A new equation was suggested to show the non-linear relationship between target variable effort and predictor variables size and productivity factor as shown in equation 2.2.

$$Effort = \frac{Complexity}{Productivity} \times Size \qquad\qquad 2.2$$

Thus the use of log linear model was justified. Before application of the linear regression model the prepossessing for the dataset was done to check the moralization of the dataset by plotting histograms of size and effort as shown in Fig 2.6 and 2.7

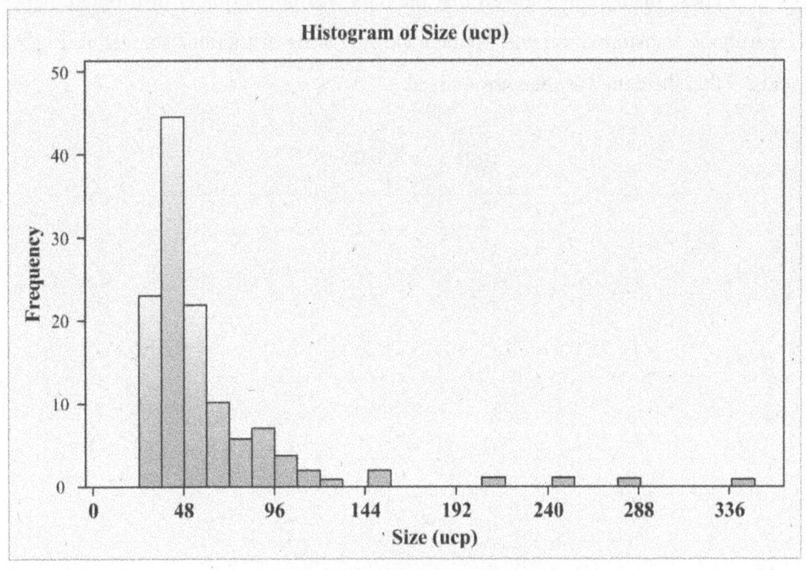

Figure 2.6: Histogram of Size

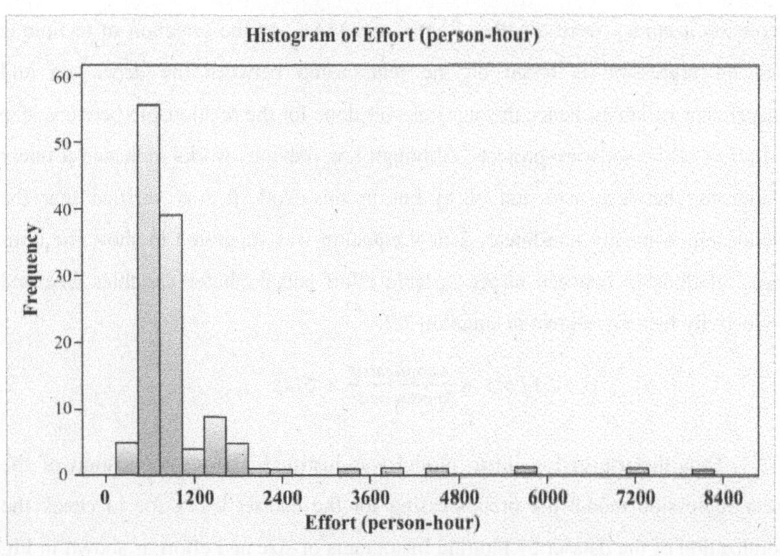

Figure 2.7: Histogram of Effort

These histograms showed that the data was not normally distributed, hence logarithmic transformation was applied and following histograms showed in Fig 2.8 and 2.9 that the data was then normalized.

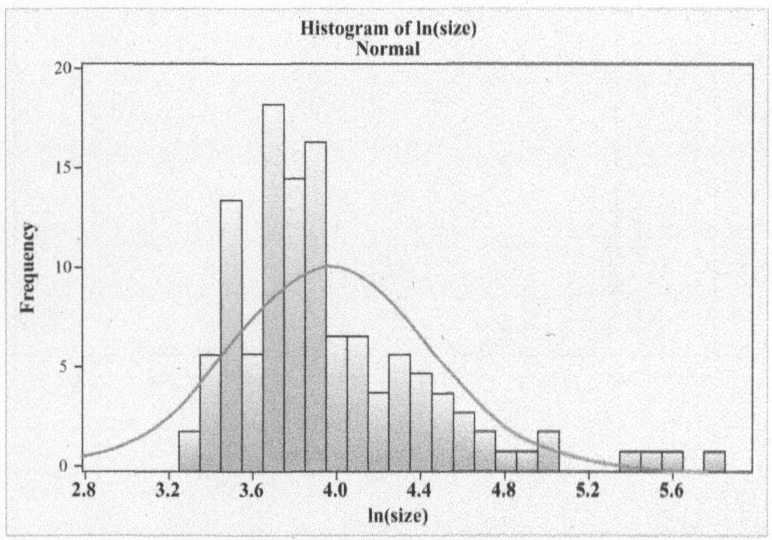

Figure 2.8: Histogram of ln(size)

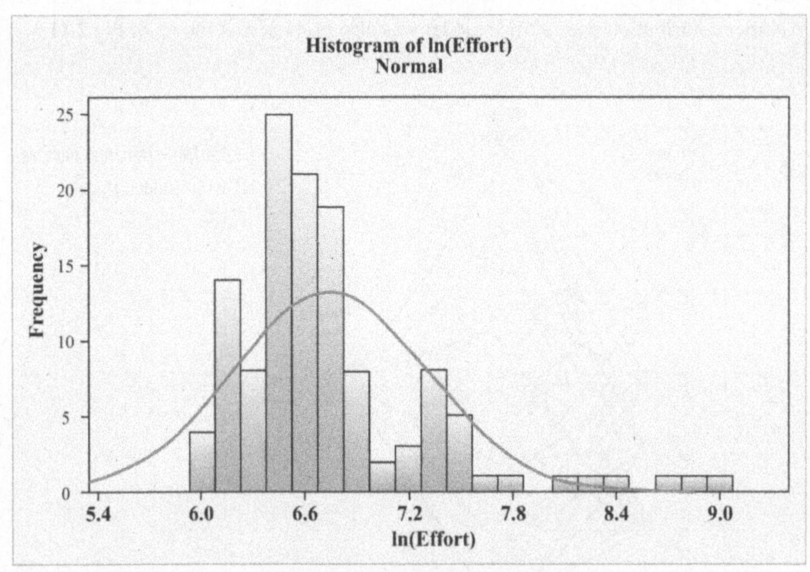

Figure 2.9: Histogram of ln (Effort)

After application of logarithmic transformation, fuzzy logic was used to tune the value of productivity factor as shown in fig. 2.10

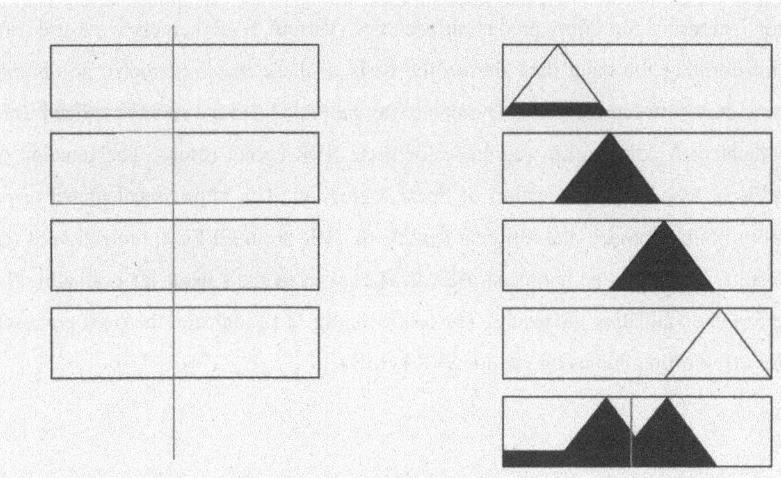

Figure 2.10: Fuzzy Inference System

Another contribution was, a MLP model was also proposed as shown in Fig 2.11

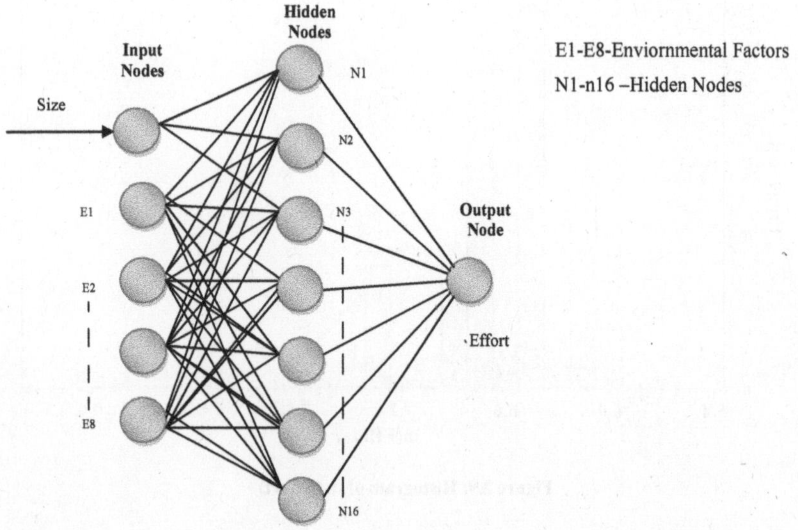

Figure 2.11: Multi-Layer Perceptron Model

(Satapathy *et al.*, 2014) suggested Support Vector Machine based technique for increasing the effort prediction accuracy. Various SVR kernels were used for transforming the input data and on the basis of these transformations, an optimal boundary between the probable outputs was generated and the results obtained were indicated. A comparison was made for these SVR-kernel results. The function of SVR is based on computation of linear regression. The effort is calculated using story point approach and different kernels of SVR are used for optimization of the results. The proposed approach used dataset given in Zia's work for evaluating the effort and validating the results. The following fig. 2.12 indicates the steps proposed for effort estimation using various SVR kernels.

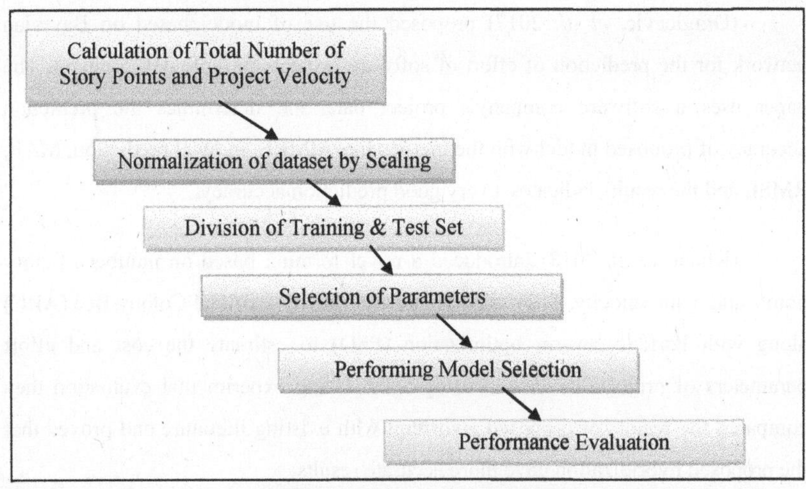

Figure 2.12: Effort Estimation Steps

The following table 2.1 displays the results suggested for the comparison of various SVR kernels methods and showed that SVR RBF kernel gave higher accuracy and less MMRE values as compared to other kernel.

Table 2.1: Comparison of Errors and Prediction Accuracy Obtained Using Various SVR Kernels

Kernel Used	MMRE Value	PRED Value
Linear	0.1492	90.81%
Polynomial	0.4350	68.73%
RBF	0.0747	95.90%
Sigmoid	0.1929	89.76%

(López-Martín, 2015) discussed the issues which comes when soft computing models are applied for prediction of the development effort. The accuracy of prediction was compared for various models based on neural network and statistical regression. The study used a published dataset containing function point as predictor variable depicting the size of project and actual effort. The results in the paper indicated that the accuracy of estimation for neural network models were better than that of regression based mathematical model.

(Dragicevic, *et al*. 2017) proposed the use of model based on Bayesian network for the prediction of effort of software projects in agile development. The paper uses a software company's project data and determines the prediction accuracy of proposed model with the metrics like MMRE, m level prediction, MAE, RMSE and the results indicates a very good prediction accuracy.

(Khuat, *et al*, 2018) introduced a novel formula based on number of story points and team velocity. They applied an ensemble of Artificial Colony Bee (ABC) along with Particle Swarm optimization (PSO) to estimate the cost and effort parameters of projects developed using agile. Using experimental evaluation they compared the results of proposed algorithm with existing literature and proved that the proposed hybridization gave more accurate results.

(Weflen, 2018) analysed and worked on the Kanban model of Agile development by proposing a Bayesian Belief Network based model for predicting the backlog completion time. Backlog is a document which is prepared by agile team containing all the requirements which are pending and needs to be met by the team. The model is used to access the factors which influences the backlog items completion time. Kanban is a model which includes all the visual practices for displaying the progress and pending tasks by using a display board known as backlog, Various columns on the display board shows the status of the pending tasks and on the basis of priority, new tasks are also added to the backlog board. As the work progress the tasks move between the columns, for which a probabilistic model was suggested. The model estimates the lead time which signifies the starting time of a task on the backlog considering all the factors which impacts the movement of the tasks on the board. An influence diagram is used to model the probabilistic relationship between the factors influencing the tasks and its lead completion time. Fig 2.13 shows the proposed model in the research.

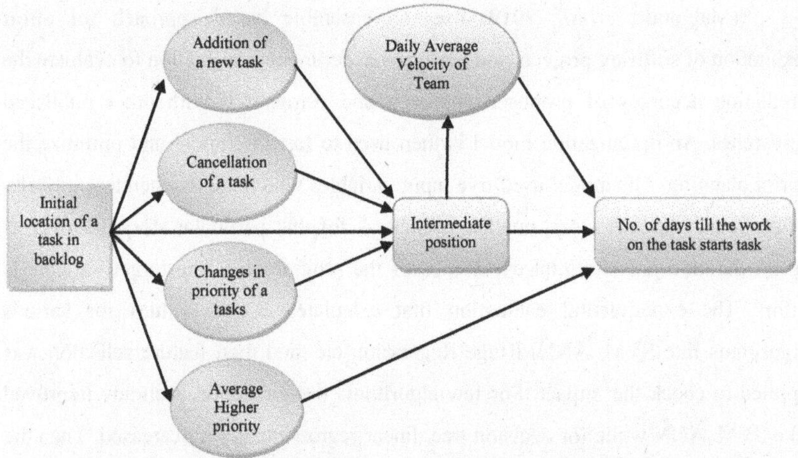

Figure 2.13: Influence Diagram showing the Factors Influencing Movement of a Task in Backlog Till Work on it Starts

The model was tested over a dataset containing the number of story points, the number of tasks cancelled and re-prioritized while the task under observation is in the backlog, the user requirements completed in a day and the number of newly added tasks. The results showed prominent results as it showed that tasks with higher priority were completed first. By estimating the completion time of the task, its correct and optimised position in the backlog can be judged. Thus the position of the estimated task was also decided by using the discrete cumulative function. Thus the model reduced the effort required for estimating the completion time of the tasks by showing the results as probabilistic forecasts.

(Zakrani, *et al.*, 2018) proposes a new and improved model for software project's effort estimation. The model applies support vector regression along with optimisation using Grid search. For applying Grid search, the parameters like type, kernel function, complexity values, kernel parameter and Epsilon values were tuned and then 5 fold cross validation was used. It also demonstrates that the result obtained on this paper outperforms the methods suggested in recent relevant literature in terms of various performance evaluation metrics.

(Malgonde, *et al.*, 2019) uses an ensemble based approach for effort estimation of software projects and performs experimental evaluation to evaluate the prediction accuracy of proposed approach and compare it with other published researches. An optimization model is then used to test the model and optimize the sprint planning. The model used five input variables which are independent: priority of particular the user story, number of subtask for that particular story, its size, its sprint duration and the total experience of the programmer. The target variable is effort. The experimental evaluation first calculated RMSE values for various algorithms like SVM, ANN, Ridge Regression etc. and then feature selection was applied to check the impact. For few algorithms the prediction accuracy improved like SVM, ANN while for decision tree, linear regression etc. it decreased. Then the weights were normalized to propose an ensemble technique and the results of proposed technique were compared with other popular ensemble technique. The following results were shown which deduced that the proposed technique performed better as compared to other algorithms.

Table 2.2: Comparison of Ensemble Techniques

Algorithm	MAE (mean absolute error	MBE (mean balanced error)	RMSE (root mean square error)
Ensemble Prediction (EP)	7.845	2.961	11.906
Average (AVG)	7.877	3.059	11.631
Extra Trees (ET)	8.578	3.536	12.369
Random Forest (RF)	8.508	3.515	12.021
Gradient Boosting (GB)	8.657	3.489	12.535
Ada Boost (AB)	8.992	3.762	12.773
Stacking (ST)	9.188	3.690	14.327

(Arora *et al.*, 2020) in their systematic literature review studied various literature available related to machine learning estimation approached used in Scrum projects. The work farmed certain research questions, and after selecting various relevant studies related to each research question, summarized their observations and discussed the research gaps and scope for the researchers. The questions framed were which ML model is usually used for estimation of software projects developed using SCRUM, do ML models outperform non ML models, what is the estimation accuracy of ML models, what is the role of meta heuristic algorithms, are ensemble techniques better, what are the factors affecting estimation. The observations included that a wide variety of algorithms based on machine learning techniques are used for effort estimation of SCRUM projects like Bayesian Networks, Support Vector Machines, PSO, Neural Networks and many others and further it was quoted that the expert estimation models often suffers from individual bias, hence normally ML models have better prediction accuracy as compared to other non ML models. It was further concluded that after comparison of all the studies, the firework optimized neural network technique gave minimum error in prediction. The following graph as shown in Fig. 2.14 was plotted to compare the MMRE values for all the algorithms used till 2020.

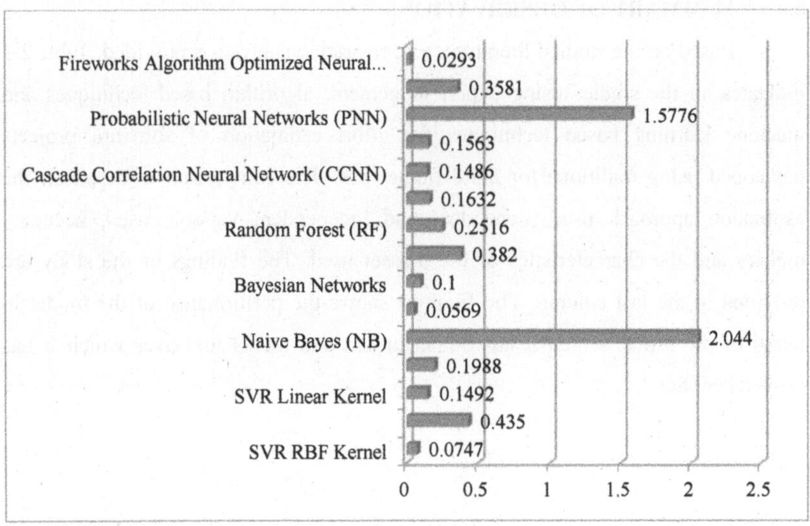

Figure 2.14: Comparison of MMRE values for Evaluating Accuracy of ML Techniques

The other observations were regarding the use of meta-heuristic algorithms and ensemble algorithms in the effort estimation and it was inferred that very less work has been done in this area so this was considered as a research gap in the area. The work which included these algorithms deduced that they give better prediction accuracy as compared to individual algorithms. The unavailability of dataset was again quoted as a concern and limitation for carrying out further work in this area.

(Gultekin *et al.*, 2020) used various ML algorithms to estimate the story point value. As compared to other published works, here it was proposed that the story point values, effort values and cost predictions must be done at each iteration so that deviation observed in the previous iteration may be taken as input for better accurate prediction in the next iteration. Various algorithms like SVR, Gradient Boosting, Random Forest etc. are applied to test the accuracy in prediction on various datasets. As the project phases are considered, hence the major advantage of the proposed work is the compensation of risk emerged in one phase into another phase. The results obtained were further compared with the already published results used in story point estimations.

2.4   SUMMARY OF OBSERVATIONS

Based on the studied literature, a comparative analysis is provided. Table 2.3 indicates all the studies using expert judgement, algorithm based techniques and machine learning based techniques for effort estimation of software projects developed using traditional or agile framework. The comparison is based on the estimation approach used, dependent and independent variable used, accuracy metrics and the characteristics of the dataset used. The findings of the study are provided in the last column. The findings shows the performance of the model in terms of the model which it has outperformed and the factors over which it has proved beneficial.

Table 2.3: Comparative Analysis of the Estimation Techniques Studied

Reference	Estimation Technique	Target Variable	Predictor Variables	Accuracy Metric	Dataset Used	Findings
Haugen, 2006	Planning Poker	Effort	Story cards from predicting team	MRE(PP)=16 MRE(UGE)=23	4 projects	Planning Poker has lower prediction error as compared to unstructured group estimation
Abrahamsson et al., 2007	Regression, Neural Network	Development Effort	Weighted methods, object points	For global models: MRE(SR)=84% MRE(RBF)=63% For incremental models: MRE(SR)=57% MRE(RBF)=37%	2 commercial projects	The effort estimation by incremental models outperform the global models
Abrahamsson et al., 2011	Expert Judgement, Regression, Neural Networks,	Effort	Character count, Keyword priority	---	1337 stories (2 projects)	The structured user stories improves the effort prediction
Ziauddin et al., 2012	Statistical Model	Effort	No. of Story Points, Velocity	MMRE = 7.19%, PRED= 57.14%	21 Project Dataset	The experimental evaluation proved that model gave better prediction accuracy as compared to expert models.
Nassif et al., 2013	Fuzzy Logic, Neural Network and Multi-Layer Perceptron	Effort	Use Case Points and Productivity Factor	For small datasets MMRE(Regression)= 43.2, PRED(100)=94.7 MMRE(MLP)=27.2 PRED(100)= 97.3 For large datasets,	Primary Datasets collected through Questionnaire(1 academic, 1 industry, 1 modified published)	The results indicated that the model based on log linear regression gave better results for smaller projects while the one based on MLP gave better results for the projects requiring large effort

Study	Technique	Type	Input	Metrics	Dataset	Remarks
				MMRE(Regression)= 34.7, PRED(100)=100 MMRE(MLP)=55 PRED(100)= 87.5		
Hamouda, 2014	Multi-Layer Neural Network	Effort	Velocity, Size	MAE=12%	Four industry Projects	The metric used was Mean Absolute error which showed better results as compared to other models.
Satapathy *et al.*, 2014	SVR linear kernel, polynomial kernel, RBF kernel, sigmoid Kernel	Effort	No of story points, team velocity	MMRE (linear) =0.1492 MMRE(polynomial)= 0.4350 MMRE(RBF)=0.0747 PRED(RBF)=95.90% MMRE(sigmoid)=0.1929	21 projects	The results suggested for the comparison of various SVR kernels methods and showed that SVR RBF kernel gave higher accuracy and less MMRE values as compared to other kernel.
Ungan *et al.*, 2014	Regression	Effort	No of story points, COSMIC functional points	MMRE(CFP)=22.48, MMRE(SP)=20.15 PRED(CFP)=77.78 PRED(SP)=77.78	10 industry projects	Regression proved to give better results in COSMIC Functional points
Ungan *et al.*, 2014	Multiple Regression			MMRE(CFP)=6.29, MMRE(SP)=NA PRED(CFP)=1008 PRED(SP)=NA		For non-linear relationships
Ungan *et al.*, 2014	Curve Fit			MMRE(CFP)=20.60 MMRE(SP)=18.93 PRED(CFP)=77.78 PRED(SP)=88.89		Curve Fit gave better results for story points
López-Martín,	SLR, MLP,	Effort	Adjusted	MAR(SLR)=0.45	Datasets	The results showed that

2015	GRNN, RBFNN		Function Points	MAR(MLP)=0.32 MAR(GRNN)=0.3 MAR(RBFNN)=0.31	containing new and enhanced in enterprise environment	RBFNN can be used for effort estimation of new projects developed using 3GL and training RBFNN is faster.
Panda *et al.*, 2015	GRNN, PNN, GMDA and CCNN	Effort	Velocity, Number of story points	MMRE=0.1486, MSE=0.0059,R^2=0.9303, PRED=95.90%	21 projects	The proposed model based on ANN outperformed Zia Work in terms of increased accuracy and reduced prediction error.
Khuat *et al.*, 2016	General regression neural network (GRNN)	Effort	Velocity, Number of story points	MMRE—0.3581	21 projects	Regression (Zia's work) and PNN
Khuat *et al.*, 2016	Probabilistic neural network (PNN)	Effort	Velocity, Number of story points	MMRE—1.5776	21 projects	Zia's work
Khuat *et al.*, 2016	GMDH polynomial neural network	Effort	Velocity, Number of story points	MMRE—0.1563	21 projects	It outperformed the models GRNN and PNN
Khuat *et al.*, 2016	Cascade correlation neural network (CCNN)	Effort	Velocity, Number of story points	MMRE—0.1486	21 projects	It outperformed the models GRNN, PNN, GMDHPNN
Khuat *et al.*, 2018	Extended ABC– PSO algorithm	Effort	Number of story points, Velocity	MMRE—0.0569	21 projects	It outperformed the models ABC -PSO, GRNN, PNN, GMDHPNN, CCNN

Zakrani *et al.*, 2018	SVR-RBF-GS	Effort	Number of story points, Velocity	MMRE-0.1640	21 projects	It outperformed the models SVM-RBF
Malgonde, *et al.*, 2019	Ensemble	Effort per story	Priority, no of subtasks, size, developed experience, sprint	MAE=8.167, RMSE=9.243	503 stories, 24 projects	Ensemble based technique improves prediction accuracy
Gultekin *et al.*,2020	Multi Layer Perceptron	Effort per story	No of issues as start, initial velocity, no of issues added, added velocity, to-do velocity	PRED=92.52% MAE=7.48	5 projects with 3233 issues	Machine learning technique based models performed better as compared to non-ML models.
Gultekin *et al.*,2020	SVR-RBF	Effort per story		PRED=97.73% MAE=2.27		
Gultekin *et al.*,2020	Gradient Boosting	Effort per story		PRED=99.8% MAE=0.2		This model gave highest accuracy
Gultekin *et al.*,2020	Random Forest	Effort per story		PRED=97.8% MAE=2.2		

CHAPTER 3
BACKGROUND TECHNIQUES USED IN PROPOSED WORK

CHAPTER 3

BACKGROUND TECHNIQUES USED IN PROPOSED WORK

The proposed research work also studies and analyses certain Machine Learning techniques and then proposes an ensemble of these. The following machine learning techniques have been studied as part of background study and their impact on the estimation of parameters for agile projects have been observed in this work. The suggested work also compares the results of the proposed work with the existing literature using below mentioned techniques.

3.1 LINEAR REGRESSION

Regression is the easiest of the machine learning techniques used for predictive analysis. The regression technique takes a training dataset $\{(x_1,y_1),...(x_i,y_i)\} \subset \chi * R$. Here, χ indicates the input pattern space and finds the function f(x) which optimizes the training data. Regression models are suggested in literature for predicting the effort of the software projects measured in man-hours. A line of separation is identified for maximising the squared error summation on the training data. (Pedregosa, 2011). The following figure 3.1 shows the line of regression

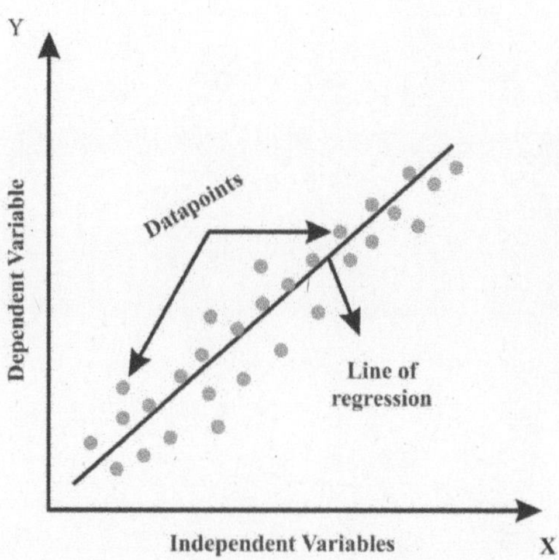

Figure 3.1: Linear Regression

3.2 LOGISTIC REGRESSION

The application of Logistic Regression is for the binary target variable values.. It uses a logistic function known as sigmoid function, whose value ranges between 0 and 1. Thus we can say that the performance of logistic regression is better in case of linearly separable data. Further, the training of the model based on logistic regression is very easy as no tuning of parameters is required. (Cournapeau, 2018)

3.3 RIDGE REGRESSION

Ridge Regression is a type of linear regression technique. Here another parameter bias is added to have better predictions. It is a regularization technique. Regularization is the solution of overfitting problem. (Cournapeau, 2018). In few cases the model performs fine on the training data but it does not give results for the test data. This problem is called overfitting. Regularization basically adds extra information to prevent the problem of overfitting. In this technique, the magnitude of the features is reduced while the same no. of features are maintained. This is done by adding a penalty or complexity term to the model. Let's consider the simple linear regression equation:

$$A = \beta_0 + \beta_1 M_1 + \beta_2 M_2 + \beta_3 M_3 + \cdots + \beta_n M_n + b \qquad 3.1$$

In the above equation, A represents the target value

$M_1, M_2, \ldots, M_n$ are the features for A.

$\beta_0, \beta_1, \ldots . \beta_n$ are the weights or magnitude related to the features, respectively. Here the magnitudes represent the bias of the model, and b indicates the intercept.

Linear regression models tries to optimize the β_0 and b to minimize the cost function. The equation for the cost function for the linear model is given below:

$$= \sum_{i=1}^{M}\left(y_i - y'_i\right)^2 = \sum_{i=1}^{M}\left(y_i - \sum_{j=o}^{n}\beta_j * Xij\right)^2 \qquad 3.2$$

Now, we will add a loss function and optimize parameter to make the model that can predict the accurate value of A. The loss function for the linear regression is called Residual sum of squares. (Pedregosa, 2011)

Ridge Regression also called as L2 Regularization adds a penalty value called Ridge Regression Penalty for altering the cost function. This is calculated by multiplying the squared weight of each feature with the lambda value as shown in following equation.

$$\sum_{i=1}^{M}(y_i - y_i')^2 = \sum_{i-1}^{M}\left(y_i - \sum_{j=0}^{n}\beta_j * x_i\right)^2 + \lambda \sum_{j=0}^{n}\beta_j^2 \qquad 3.3$$

3.4 SUPPORT VECTOR REGRESSION

Support Vector Regression is a version of Support Vector Machine which works on the minimization of structural risk through the implantation of principle of induction. The two problems faced by usage of un-normalized dataset are local minima and over-fitting. Further, a kernel function is also used and can be further optimized to improve the capability of generalization. (Satapathy, 2017) also introduced the significance of ε-SVR. Here, the prediction is done by using a ε loss function.

In SVR based on linear regression, function d(x) = (v, u) + d. Here v ∈ χ whereas x ∈ R. For non-linear regression d(x) = (v, φ(x)) + d, where φ is a non-linear function. For optimization of following problem the values of v and d are selected:

$$minimize_{w,b,\xi,\xi^*} \; \frac{1}{2}\langle w,w \rangle + C \sum_{i=1}^{l}\left(\xi_i + \xi_i^*\right), \qquad 3.4$$

$$subject \; to \; \begin{cases} \left(\langle w, \Phi(x^i)\rangle + b\right) - y_i \le \varepsilon + \xi_i, \\ y_i - \left(\langle w, \Phi(x^i)\rangle + b\right) \le \varepsilon + \xi_i, \\ \xi_i, \xi_i^* \ge 0. \end{cases} \qquad 3.5$$

For performing optimization of an objective relation, values are calculated using the slack variables ζ and ζ* and constant C.

3.5 RADIAL BASIS FUNCTION NETWORK

The Radial basis function model is defined as a feed forward type of network which generally contains a single layer which is hidden and k number of hidden centers (Prasada, 2018). The activation function is defined using basis functions. The application of activation function is done after the calculation of Euclidean distance. The final output is calculated by applying summation to the product of weights with output of activation functions from all hidden nodes.

$$y' = \sum_{i=1}^{n} \emptyset_i W_i \qquad\qquad 3.6$$

where y' is the output, w_i is the ith centre's weight and ϕ is the radial function. The architecture of RBFN is shown in Figure 3.2

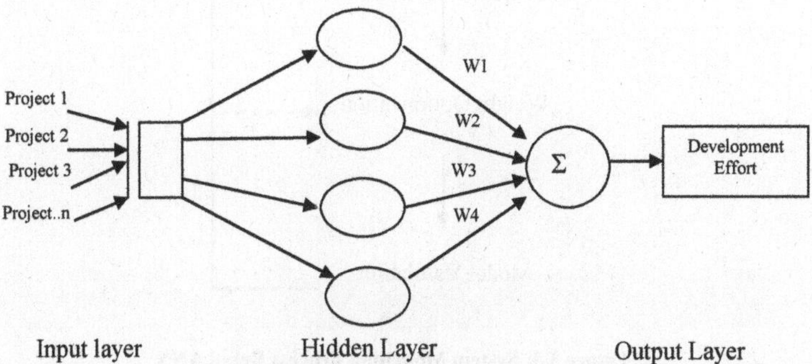

Figure 3.2: RBFN Architecture

3.6 ARTIFICIAL NEURAL NETWORK

The back propagation functions on a network of simple processing elements. The architecture is motivated by the network of biological nervous network hence it is termed as Artificial Neural Network. Every processing unit residing in the network calculates a function which is non-linear function of all the inputs supplied to it and generates an output.

$$\frac{1}{1+exp\left[-(\sum_i w_i I_i)\right]} \qquad\qquad 3.7$$

Here, $w_i I_i$ is the weighted summation of all the inputs applied to a particular processing element.

The network computes the output by propagating the inputs, passing through certain intermediate processing layers and finally to the output layer. Figure 3.3 shows the architecture of the modelling process using Artificial Neural Networks.

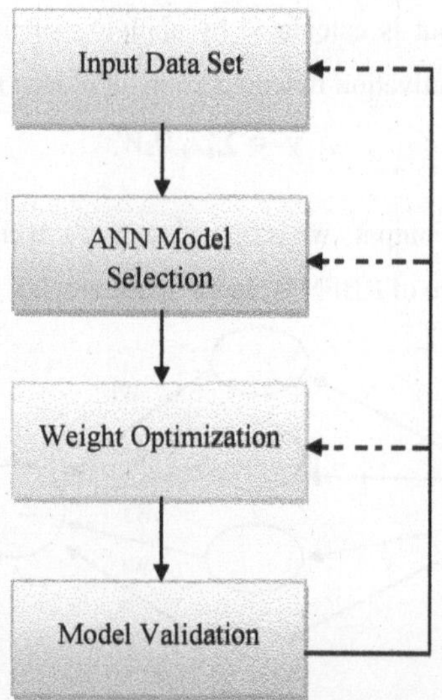

Figure 3.3: System Modelling Process Based ANN

The fundamental unit of computation in ANN is a neuron, referred to as a node or unit. In single neuron architecture, a node generates output by taking input from other nodes, where a weight is associated with every input. The weight signifies its relative importance to other inputs. The node calculates the weighted sum of all inputs and applies a function on it as shown in fig 3.4. The figure takes X1 and X2 as inputs with their corresponding weights as w1 and w2. Along with these, there is an additional input 1 whose weight is b. This input is referred to as bias. The bias basically provides a trainable constant value to every node. The function f is referred to as activation function. This activation function introduces non-linearity into the output of the node. Various activation functions are used in practice like Sigmoid, tanh, ReLU. These functions signifies the way they operates on the input. Sigmoid takes an input and transforms it to the range between 0 and 1, tanh into range -1 and 1 and ReLU replaces all negative values with zero. (Sharma, 2017) The figure 3.4 show the activation function calculation.

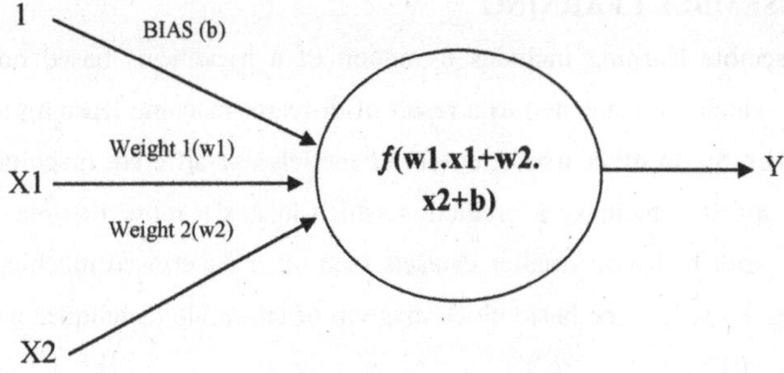

Figure 3.4: Single Neuron Architecture

Output of Node = Y = f(w1.x1+w2.x2+b)

The first neural network used was feedforward, Its architecture comprises of input layers, hidden layers and output layer containing multiple nodes i.e. input, hidden and output nodes. The nodes of adjacent layers are connected and the edges have weights associated with them. The input layer nodes pass on the information to the hidden nodes without performing any processing. The hidden layer nodes perform the computation and transfer the information to the output nodes. The feedforward network can have zero or multiple hidden layers while single input and single output layer. The output nodes transfer information to the outside world.

Two examples of feedforward networks are Single Layer Perceptron and Multi-Layer Perceptron. The Single Layer Perceptron doesn't contain any hidden layer while a Multi-Layer has one or multiple hidden layers

3.7 BACKPROPOGATION

Backpropogation algorithm is used by Multi Layer Perceptron for learning process. The learning process is referred as Backpropogation as it learns from mistakes. This is done by setting a goal of assigning correct weights for all the edges. At the first step, all the weights are assigned. For the training dataset, the ANN is activated for every input and then the output is observed. The output is then compared with the expected output and the difference i.e. the error is then back propagated to the previous layer. The weights are then adjusted according to this error. This process is repeated until the error goes below a predefined threshold value.

3.8   ENSEMBLE LEARNING

Ensemble learning includes formation of a hypothesis based on multiple hypothesis which are generated as a result of different machine learning techniques used together. So, in other words, ensemble models use different machine learning techniques together to make a prediction which makes it more flexible. This also helps it to work better on smaller datasets then other supervised machine learning models. Fig 3.5 shows the basic block diagram of ensemble techniques as given by (Malgonde, 2019).

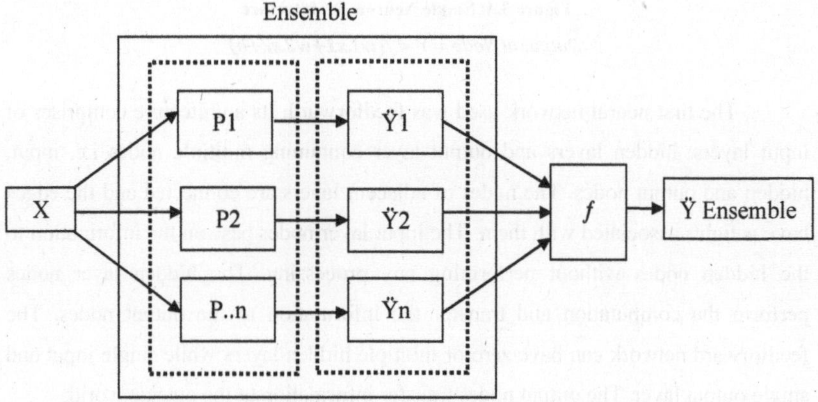

Figure 3.5: Ensemble Architecture (Malgonde, 2016)

The ensemble methods are classified as Averaging methods or Boosting methods. The Averaging methods works by averaging the predictions done by multiple estimators. The examples of averaging methods are random forest, bagging etc. The Boosting methods on the other hand, combines various weak estimators to create an effective ensemble. The single estimators are used in sequential manner to reduce the bias. Examples of boosting methods are adaboosting, gradient boosting etc. (Benalal, 2018) Following ensemble techniques have been studied and implemented in the proposed work based on their applicability validation in previously published literature

3.8.1   Ada –Boosting Regressor

Ada- Boosting algorithm is an ensemble technique which builds a strong regressor from a series of weak regressors. Initially a model is built using training data. The errors present in this model are corrected by building a second model in series. The algorithm for re increased. Ada-boosting technique initialises the dataset and for each data point, equal weights are assigned. These are provided as input to the model and the weights of the wrongly identified data points are increased. Thus it is a meta-estimator which starts applying regression on the initial dataset and then by adjusting the weights according to the current prediction error, it further fits additional regression on the same dataset. (Pedregosa, 2011) Following Fig 3.6 shows the block diagram of the model.

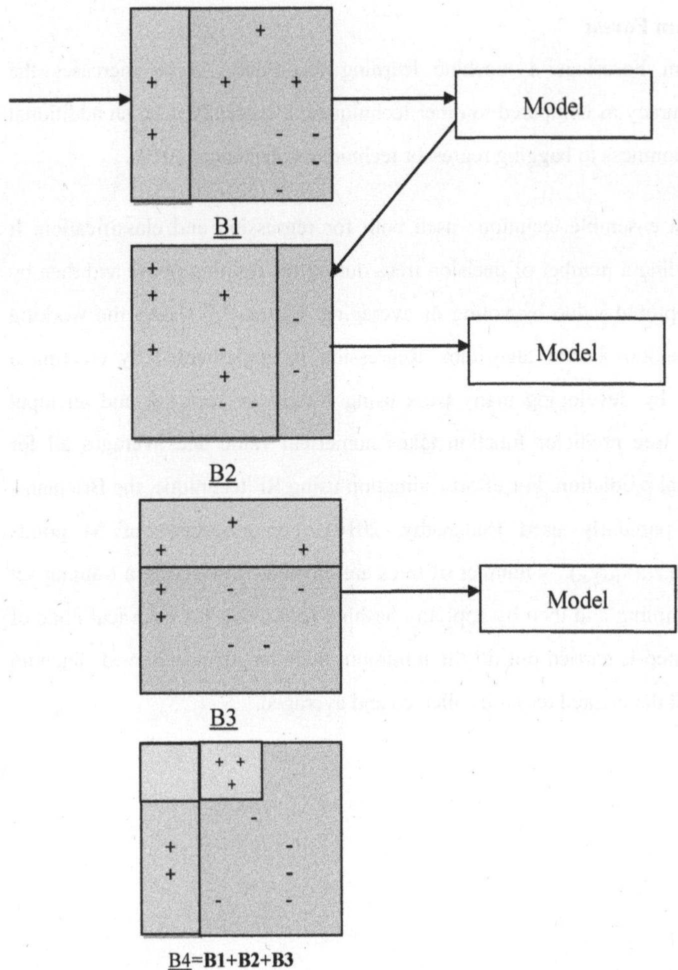

Figure 3.6: Block Diagram of Ada Boosting Regressor

3.8.2 Bagging Regressor

This is an averaging method ensemble technique which first applies regression on a random subset of the dataset to get individual predictions and then forms a final prediction by averaging or voting. This can be used to reduce the variance of decision tree predictions which is a black box estimator as it introduces randomization into the construction process of random trees and then creates an ensemble.

3.8.3 Random Forest

Random Forest is a machine learning technique, which increases the prediction accuracy as compared to other techniques. It basically adds an additional feature of randomness to bagging regressor technique (Mustapha, 2019).

It is an ensemble technique used both for regression and classification. It works by building a number of decision trees during the training phase and then by selecting an optimal value by voting or averaging. Figure 3.7 shows the working process of Random Forest algorithm. Regression is implemented by creating a random forest by developing many trees using a random vector μ and an input vector a. The tree predictor function takes numerical value and averages all for finding the final prediction. For effort estimation using RF technique, the Brieman's algorithm is popularly used (Satapathy, 2016). For a dataset of M points $(x1,y1),(x2,y2),\ldots(x_m,y_m)$, N number of trees are created by selecting a training set by random sampling and then by applying hashing repeatedly for each leaf node of the tree. The step is carried out till the minimum node length is achieved. Then an ensemble of all the created tees are collected and averaged.

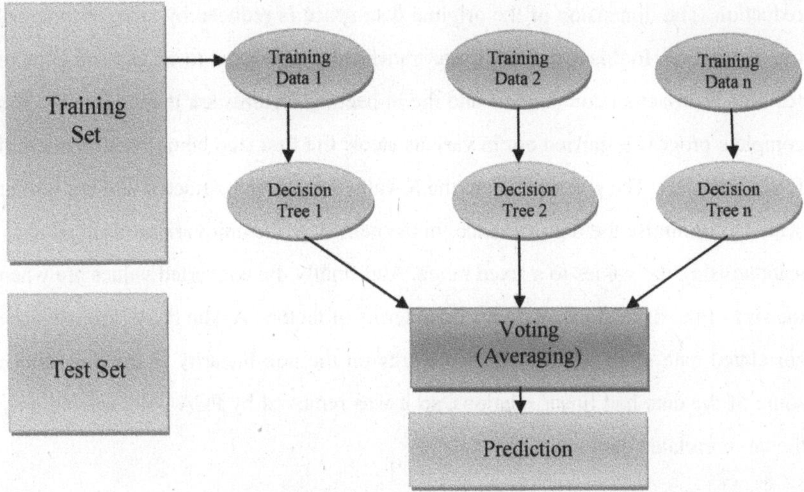

Figure 3.7: Random Forest Prediction

3.8.4   Stochastic Gradient Boosting

The SGB is an ensemble technique which calculates the final prediction by creating an ensemble of trees using randomization and by calculating the accuracy of prediction by providing the result obtained from one tree to the next tree in series.

3.8.5   Extra Trees

Extremely randomized tree is a recent machine learning technique. It is an extension of the random forest technique. The advantage pf this technique that the probability of overfitting the dataset is very less in this case. It also uses randomisation and selects a subset of features to train each tree. It uses the complete dataset to train each regression tree. The difference between extra trees and random forest is that it applies randomisation in selecting the best feature for splitting the node and also uses a bootstrapped subset for training. (Geurts, 2006)

3.9   PRINCIPAL COMPONENT ANALYSIS

PCA is basically used for reducing the feature dimensions by identifying the key attributes through reduction of the dimensions of those attribute having highest correlation with the target variable. The application of PCA has been suggested in various studies for feature extraction resulting in better prediction accuracy and error reduction. The dimension of the original data space is reduced by suing orthogonal transformation. In this technique linear transformation is used to extract some major features from actual components and the impacting features are then extracted. The complete process is carried out in various steps: the first step being identification of feature data set. The patterns where the X-values exists are extracted and are further scaled to minimise the high variance. In the next step, the unit variance is applied by standardising the values to a fixed range. And finally the converted values are when the size of the data comes out reduced in terms of factors. As the PCA eliminates the correlated data so this reduction also works on the non-linearity in the data. Since some of the data had linear relations, so it was removed by PCA, thus leaving only the un- correlated data.

CHAPTER 4
METHODOLOGY USED

The methodology used to attain the above mentioned objectives has been divided into two phases each of which contain various progressive steps.

Phase 1

Extensive Literature survey Analysis of agile development process and estimation algorithms Collection and analysis of various datasets related to the projects developed using agile methodology

Phase 2

Identification and application of suitable machine learning model for estimation Measurement of accuracy in estimation process using measurement metrics

The proposed techniques for both effort and cost estimation of agile project basically follows the application of story point approach which is widely used in the agile estimation and further applies various ML techniques for the optimization and validation of the results obtained.

4.1   STORY POINT APPROACH

The Story Point Approach is widely used for estimating the cost and effort of the projects developed specifically using the Agile process. The effort of a project is calculated by estimating the size of the software. In SCRUM, the user stories define the user requirements and the story points describe the measure for the user stories. The size of the project is measured using number of story points. But while estimating the effort of the project, velocity of the team also plays a key role. The velocity of a team is defined by the number of stories that the team successfully delivers in a particular iteration termed as Sprint. The size of a user story is determined by taking into consideration the complexity of the requirement.

(Ziauddin, 2012) suggested various scales which define the complexity of a user story relatively. The user story having the complexity value 1 depicts a very small story which requires very less effort while with the value 5 depicts a very large story requiring five times more effort as compared to the previous one. Further the story with value 1 requires a basic skill set while one with 5 requires an advanced set of skilled team professionals for successful completion.

Using the complexity and size vectors, effort of a specific story is calculated as:

$$ES_i = \text{Complexity} \times \text{Size} \qquad\qquad 4.1$$

The summation of all these individual effort values gives the total effort of the project. It is calculated as:

$$Effort\ (E) = \sum_{i-1}^{n}(ES)_i \qquad\qquad 4.2$$

The Velocity which is defined by the backlog a team can handle in a particular Sprint is calculated by:

$$V_i = \frac{Units\ of\ Effort}{Sprint\ Duration} \qquad\qquad 4.3$$

According to (Ziauddin, 2012), the two factors which may decrease the team's velocity are the Friction Force (FF) and the Dynamic Force (DF). The Friction Force brings down the productivity of the team and the Dynamic Force lowers the pace of the team.

Total Friction Force (FF) is determined by calculating the multiplication of all the four friction factors which are the composition of the team, the process followed, the environmental factors and the team dynamics. All these frictional factors may have a significant impact on the productivity of the team, hence they must be eliminated or at least reduced.

Total Dynamic Force (DF) is determined by calculating the product of all nine dynamic factors. These factors are variable and as they are unpredictable so they must be made consistent to have better velocity of the team. These factors are the changes in the team, new tools introduced, third party defective tools, additional responsibilities of the team members, person issues of the team members, non-responsive stake holders, unclear customer requirements, constantly changing requirements and team relocation. Thus all these forces are unexpected and hence may affect the velocity significantly when they are cumulatively present.

The negative change of the velocity defined as Deceleration is then calculated by applying the product operation on values of Friction and Dynamic Forces

$$D = FR \times DF \qquad\qquad 4.4$$

The final Team Velocity is determined by adjusting the velocity in a predictable range. It is represented by V and is calculated by following:

$$V = (V_i)^D \qquad\qquad 4.5$$

The completion time of the project is determined by:

$$T = \frac{\sum_{i-1}^{n} ES_i}{V_i^D} \times {}^1\!/_{WD}\, months \qquad\qquad 4.6$$

where T denotes the completion time and WD indicates the number of working days per month.

The Development Cost is determined by:

$$COST = 1.681 \times Team\ Salary \times Time \qquad\qquad 4.7$$

where TS is measured in dollors and Time in Months.

The normalized values of effort and cost are then calculated by supplying the input argument values of story points and the final velocity of the agile projects.

4.2   PROPOSED APPROACH

The proposed approach uses a dataset of 21 rows taken from previously published work by (Ziauddin, 2012). The dataset consists of various fields for effort calculation of 21 projects developed by a software firm using agile development methodology. The dataset consists of the actual effort, velocity, Sprint size, work days and other relevant fields for calculation of effort in man-hours.

To implement the proposed techniques, dataset given by (Ziauddin, 2012) is used. There are 21 rows and 3 columns in the dataset comprising of data of 21 agile projects. The data in the first column are the number of story points required to complete the project, the next column contains the initial or the raw velocity and the last column contains the actual effort required to successfully complete the project.

Machine Learning Models takes number of story points and project velocity as input and the output is the predicted effort value which represents the time required to complete the project (Satapathy, 2014).The following pre-processing steps are performed during experimental evaluation

Step-1: Statistical Analysis of the Dataset: The statistical analysis is performed as part of pre-processing. This step checks the data normalisation as only normalised data can be supplied to any machine learning technique. To check whether the data is normalized or not, various statistical measures like standard deviation, skewness and kurtosis are determined. The Table 4.1 indicates the various statistical values calculated with respect to the actual effort. The figure 4.1 shows the relationship among the no. of story points and actual effort. Further, for validation is done by plotting a histogram for the values of number of story points. As the measures and the histogram indicates that the data is not normalized, so scaling is performed. As part of the scaling, the values are transformed to normalise the data. Most frequently used transformation technique is taking a natural logarithm to make the values smaller and bring the data values closer.

Table 4.1: Parameters of Actual Effort

Mean Value	56.42857
Lowest Value	21
Highest Value	112
Median Value	52
Std. Deviation	26.17742
Skewness	0.562172
Kurtosis	-1.0676

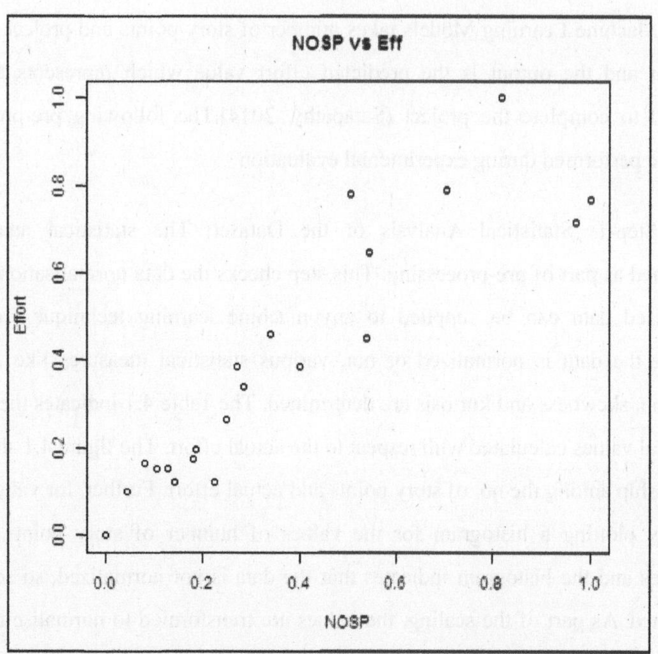

Figure 4.1: Relationship among Effort and Story Points

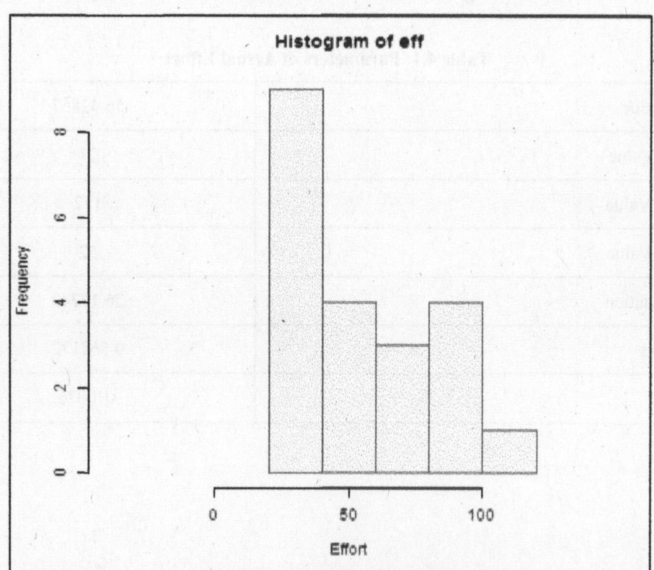

Figure 4.2: Histogram of Effort

Step-2: Division of Data Set: Here the data set is divided into training set and testing set using n-fold cross validation approach.

The next steps that are the selection of parameters and performance evaluation techniques are done depending on the model used to optimize the results. (Satapathy, 2014)

The dataset is analysed on the basis of various descriptive statistical measures as shown in Table 4.2

Table 4.2: Descriptive Statistical Measures of Dataset (21 Projects)

	Effort	Vi	D	V	Sprint Size	Work days	Team Salary	Act Time
count	21.000000	21.000000	21.000000	21.000000	21.0	21.000000	21.000000	21.000000
mean	163.714286	4.071429	0.780381	3.023810	10.0	21.952381	246190.476190	56.428571
std	82.743062	0.325796	0.071028	0.438069	0.0	0.218218	46419.413016	26.177417
min	62.000000	3.700000	0.646000	2.400000	10.0	21.000000	190000.000000	21.000000
25%	101.000000	3.900000	0.742000	2.800000	10.0	22.000000	220000.000000	35.000000
50%	137.000000	4.000000	0.758000	2.900000	10.0	22.000000	250000.000000	52.000000
75%	211.000000	4.200000	0.833000	3.200000	10.0	22.000000	250000.000000	80.000000
max	339.000000	4.900000	0.903000	4.200000	10.0	22.000000	400000.000000	112.000000

Next, to analyze the data and check the normalization as well as information about outliers, we have observed the box plots of all data items. Figure 4.3 depicts the data distribution using box-plots for the dependent and independent variables.

Next, the correlation among the attributes is plotted using a heat-map to check the dependence of individual variables on the dependent variable. Figure 4.4 shows the heat-map of the attributes.

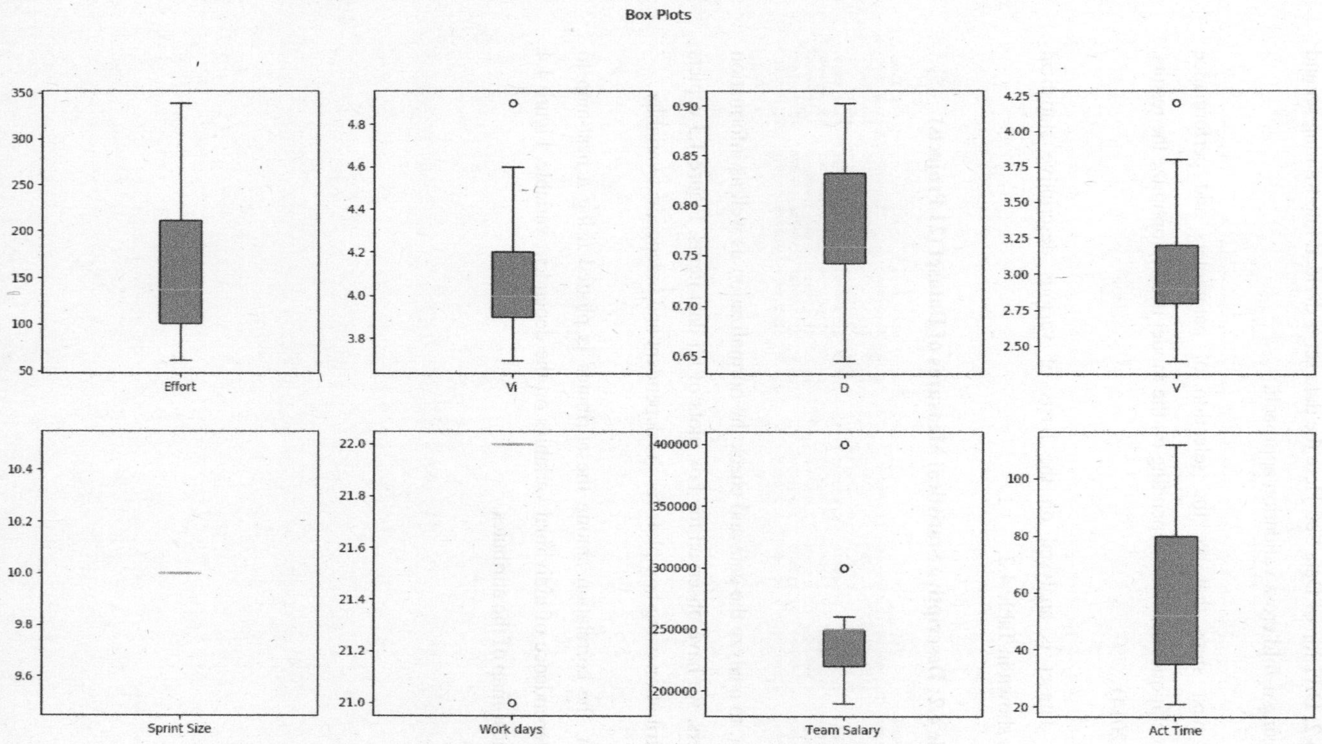

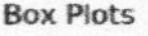

Box Plots

Figure 4.3: Box-plots of Predictor Variables

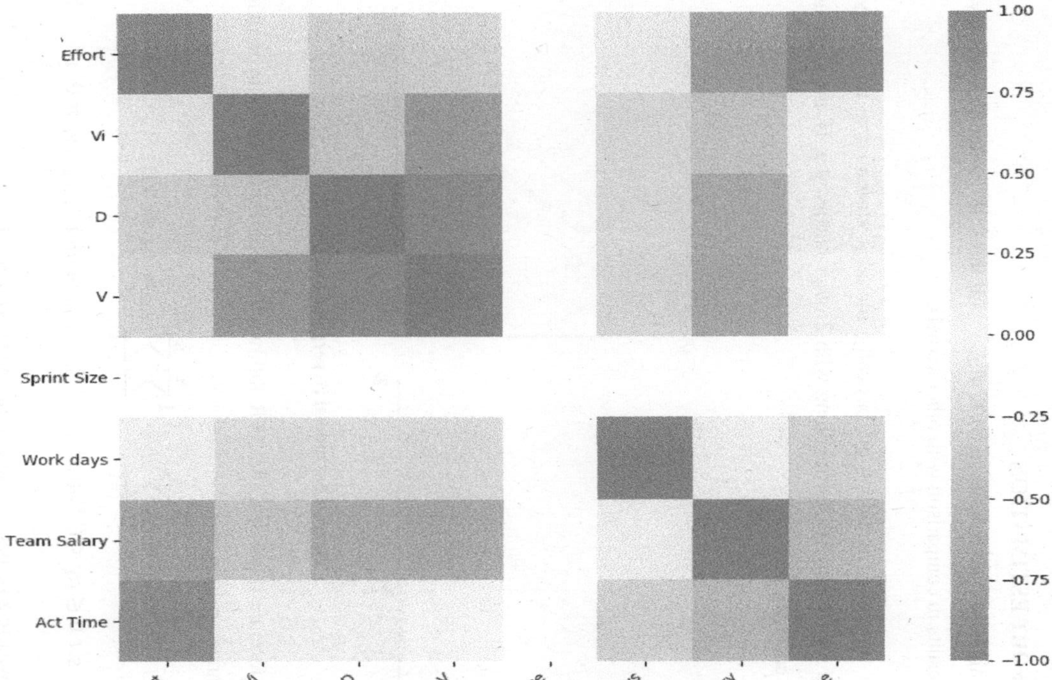

Figure 4.4: Heat-map of Attributes

The darker the blue colour higher is the correlation, and the darker the brown colour higher is negative correlation. Negative correlation implies that when one value increases the value of the other decreases.

4.3   EFFORT ESTIMATION

In this work, we have used SVR along with the RBF kernel as it has given improved results in comparison with other kernels.

The proposed methodology basically includes customizing the Support Vector Regressor with RBF kernel along with 2 other factors, that is, the slope and the biasing constant.

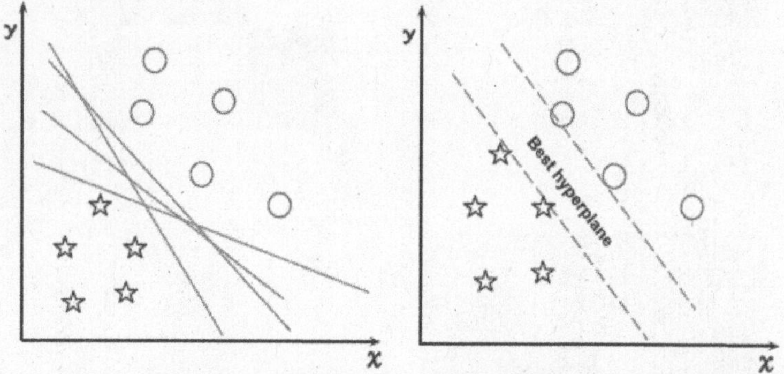

Figure 4.5: Optimal Hyperplane using SVM

So, as per formula if we see, the SVR follows the optimization of its hyperplane using Lagrange's principle –

$$\text{maximize}_{\alpha} \sum_{i=1}^{n} \alpha_i - \frac{1}{2} \sum_{i=1}^{n} \sum_{j=1}^{n} \alpha_i \alpha_j y_i y_j \left(X_i^T . X_j \right)$$

$$s.t\ 0 \leq \alpha_i \leq C\ For\ all\ i = 1,2, \ldots \ldots \ldots, n\ and\ \sum_{i=1}^{n} \alpha_i y_i = 0 \qquad 4.8$$

And when we use a kernel, the same function gets changed to-

$$\text{maximize}_{\alpha} \sum_{i=1}^{n} \alpha_i - \frac{1}{2} \sum_{i=1}^{n} \sum_{j=1}^{n} \alpha_i \alpha_j y_i y_j K \left(X_i^T . X_j \right)$$

$$s.t\ 0 \leq \alpha_i \leq C\ For\ all\ i = 1,2, \ldots \ldots \ldots, n\ and\ \sum_{i=1}^{n} \alpha_i y_i = 0 \qquad 4.9$$

Now, for RBF kernel the function follows as:

$$K(X_1, X_2) = exponent(-\gamma \|X_1 - X_2\|^2) \qquad 4.10$$

If we consider the final prediction made by the model to be Y', then as per our methodology, we have 2 more factors included:

$$Y' \Rightarrow (Theta * Y') + B \qquad 4.11$$
$$Theta \Rightarrow Slope \qquad 4.12$$
$$B \Rightarrow Biasconstant \qquad 4.13$$

To optimize these two factors, we have used neural network technique to find the optimal point.

On analyzing RBF response to our dataset, we found that the prediction trend of our model lacks two parameters which are key components to our linear models. These two components are slope and constant. So, our methodology includes customizing the normal RBF response to follow along the above mentioned components. Moreover, to get the most optimized result for our integrated model, we have used a small perceptron model to predict the slope and intercept constant value for the model. Also, we have used various evaluation metrics to check the accuracy. The algorithm and flowchart of the proposed technique is shown in the following figures.

4.4 ALGORITHM OF THE PROPOSED APPROACH

Algorithm

Step 1: Statistical Analysis of the Dataset: To check whether the data is normalized or not, an analysis of the dataset based on certain statistical measures is carried out..

Step 2: Dataset Transformation: This step takes input parameters as the number of story points and velocity and scaled them within the range [0,1], If A is the dataset and a is an element of the data set, then the value of a after scaling is calculated as

$$a' = \frac{a - \min(A)}{\max(A) - \min(A)}$$

Step 3: Partitioning of dataset into train & test set

Step 4: Model Building & Optimization:

a.   Predicting outputs using SVM model and applying RBF Kernel (Eq. 4.8,4.9 & 4.10)

b.   Putting predicted output as X in our formula, Y = Theta * X + B, we will train our neural network to find value for theta and B (Eq. 4.11,4.12 & 4.13)

Step 5: Cross validation

Step 6: Calculate prediction accuracy and error rates.

Using our derived values to get the final prediction and calculating error use different error metrics.

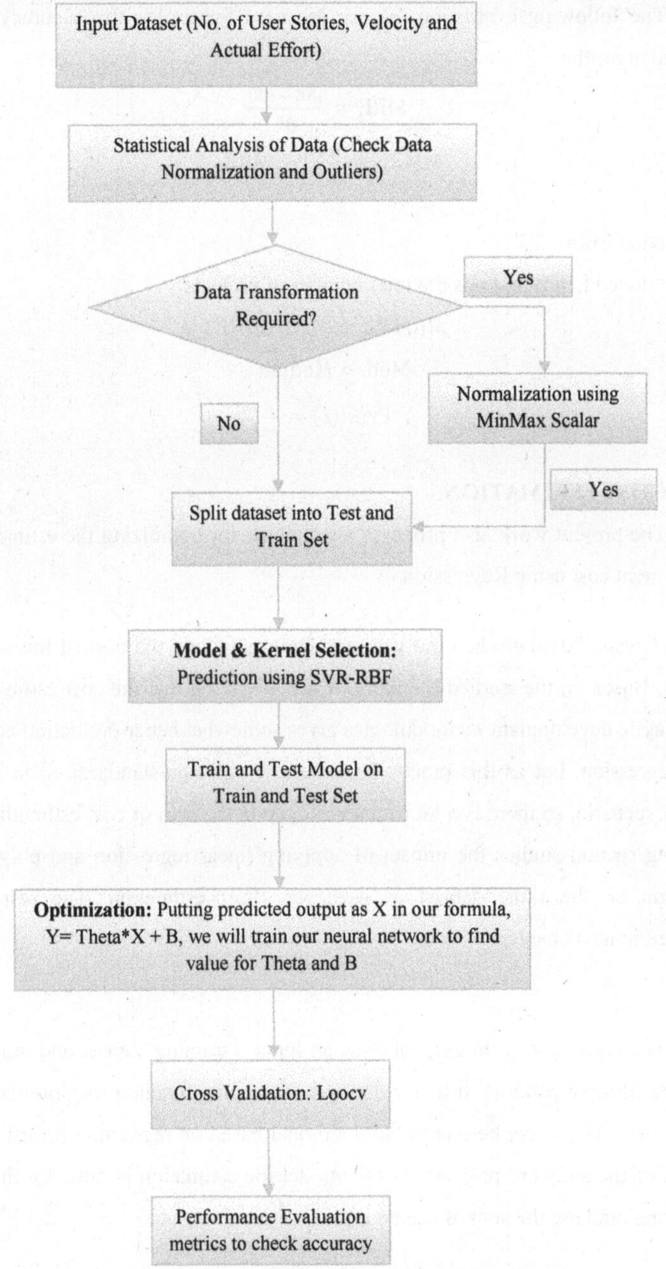

Figure 4.6: Flowchart of Proposed Approach

4.6   EVALUATION METRICS

The following evaluation metrics are used for testing the accuracy of the proposed algorithm.

$$MRE = \frac{|AE - PE|}{AE} \qquad\qquad 4.14$$

$$MMRE = \frac{1}{p}\sum_{k=1}^{p} MRE_k \qquad\qquad 4.15$$

where

AE = Actual Effort,

PE = Predicted Effort and p is the total number of projects

$$MdMRE = Med.(MRE) \qquad\qquad 4.16$$

$$Med. = Median$$

$$Pred(l) = \frac{p}{m} \qquad\qquad 4.17$$

4.7   COST ESTIMATION

The present work also proposes a technique for optimizing the estimation of development cost using Regression.

(Owais, 2016) studied the various factors affecting the cost of the software projects. Based on the studied literature, it was observed that the cost estimation in case of agile development methodologies gives somewhat better prediction accuracy using regression, but as this practical measure is still non-standardised in various industry scenario, so there is a lot of research gap in the area of cost estimation. The following section studies the impact of applying linear regression and polynomial regression on the same dataset as used for effort estimation. The results are published in next chapter.

4.7.1   Linear Regression

The regression technique takes as an input a training dataset and maps it to the space of input patterns. It then calculates a mapping function for optimizing the training data. The intent here is to build a model based on regression for estimating the cost of the software projects. In this model the estimation is done by finding a line for maximizing the sum of square error on the training set.

4.7.2 Polynomial Regression

Polynomial Regression is a regression technique where the relationship between the target variable and the predictor variables is modelled as a polynomial of degree n. It is normally applied for non-linear relationships between independent and dependent variables, but as the regression coefficients are linear, hence this is considered as a special case of linear regression.

Since it provides a better fit even in case of linear relationship, hence this has been used in this work to show the prediction accuracy.

4.8 FEATURE EXTRACTION BY PCA

Principal Component Analysis is a supervised linear technique, used dimensionality reduction. It works by identifying the key features having maximum impact on the target variable using Correlation Calculation of the features. An orthogonal transformation is used to map the original data set to dimensionally reduced data space. This work proposes the evaluation of significance in the use of feature extraction for the small size of data set available. The methodology used by PCA follows the following steps

Step-1: Pre-processing of the dataset –. As there is a high variance in the data values so, scaling must be performed to transform the data into a limited range. The standard scaling procedure removes the mean. Then scaling is performed to unit variance. If the range has higher variance, then the estimator goes wrong in learning from the values.

Step 2: Transformation after PCA- Once the PCA is applied, the size of the data is reduced column-wise that is the factors are minimised. The PCA technique maximizes the non-linearity by removing the correlated data. This is done by identifying the linear relationship between the features and removing the linearly related data

Step 3: Determining Covariance- The most important feature is determined by checking the relationship amongst various features. For this, the covariance matrix is constructed. The Eigen values and vectors are also determined for identifying the principal components. The Eigen values represents the weights of the feature and is used for finding the highest correlated feature. The covariance calculation is carried out by performing following steps

i)   The average mean is calculated.

ii)   The elements are then subtracted from the mean value to construct the covariance matrix.

iii) The Eigen values are then determined by using the covariance matrix Thes sorting of these eigen values is performed in decremented order and number of dimensions intended are retrieved.

iv)   The first k-eigen values are used to transform n dimensions to k.

The correlation matrix and the eigen values are shown in Table 4.3 and 4.4 and Figure 4.7 shows the covariance plotting,

Table 4.3: Covariance Matrix

Effort	Initial Velocity	Ideal Days	Team Velocity	Sprint Size	Work days	Total Salary of the team	Actual Time	Covariance
Effort	6846.414	4.876429	2.176514	12.077143	0	-1.914286	2813357	1979.028571
Initial Velocity	4.876429	0.106143	0.009436	0.109714	0	0.018571	6385.714	-0.452143
Ideal Days	2.176514	0.009436	0.005045	0.02762	0	0.003969	2088.024	0.153729
Team Velocity	12.07714	0.109714	0.02762	0.191905	0	0.02619	13345.24	0.169286
Sprint Size	0	0	0	0	0	0	0	0
Work days	-1.914286	0.018571	0.003969	0.02619	0	0.047619	-690.4762	-1.778571
Total Salary	2813357	6385.714286	2088.02381	13345.2381	0	-690.47619	2154762000	641714.2857
Actual Time	1979.029	-0.452143	0.153729	0.169286	0	-1.778571	641714.3	685.257143

Table 4.4: Eigen Vectors

Effort	Vi	D	V	Sprint Size	Work days	Total Salary of the team	Actual Time
Effort	0.001305647	-0.938402	-0.345427	-0.007258	-0.003866	0.003409	-0.00007409916
Vi	0.000002963531	0.00113	-0.013718	0.750099	0.107065	0.636479	-0.1435032
D	0.0000009690264	0.000189	-0.003373	0.043125	-0.037789	-0.261757	-0.9634231
V	0.000006193361	0.001762	-0.023316	0.657515	-0.193601	-0.692069	0.2251387
Sprint Size	0	0	0	0	0	0	0
Work days	-0.0000003204425	0.000416	-0.015228	0.049574	0.974419	-0.217448	0.02313212
Team Salary	0.9999991	0.001328	0.000172	-0.000004	0.000003	0.000001	-0.00000004515743
Act Time	0.0002978126	-0.345535	0.937926	0.025603	0.011014	-0.011112	0.0003821539

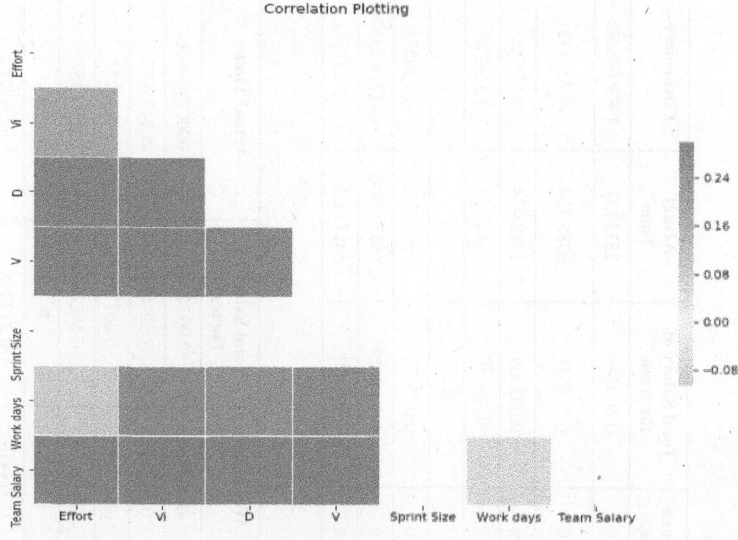

Figure 4.7: Correlation Plotting

Implementation of the proposed methodology:

All the above mentioned methodologies and concepts are implemented using Python and the results are indicated in next chapter. The PCA is applied before the application of every implementation to evaluate its impact on the accuracy of prediction. Similarly the proposed techniques for cost and effort estimations are applied and the results are shown as indicated in the next chapter.

CHAPTER 5
RESULTS & OBSERVATIONS

CHAPTER 5
RESULTS & OBSERVATIONS

This chapter shows the results obtained after applying the proposed methodology for effort and cost estimation of software projects. Following sections discusses the results of both proposed approaches along with the impact of another concept PCA which is used for feature extraction

5.1   RESULTS OBTAINED FOR PROPOSED APPROACH FOR EFFORT ESTIMATION

After the experimental evaluation is done using Python, we analyse the output and we plot the graphs showing the predicted vs. actual effort values. The graphs are generated first after application of RBF kernel and then after the optimization using backpropogation. The following observations are made:

If we observe the output of using, SVR with RBF kernel, we get the output as shown in fig 5.1:

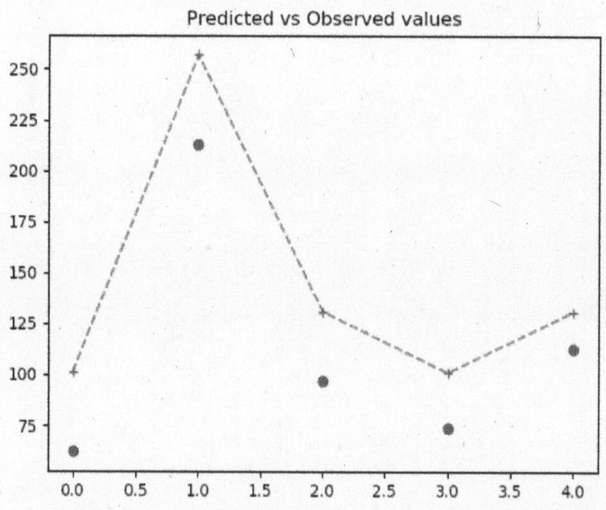

Figure 5.1: Graph depicting Predicted Vs. Actual Effort using SVR-RBF

As we can clearly see that the prediction results are as per trend but has a bias value added to it, so if we remove the bias term from it, we get the result as shown in fig 5.2

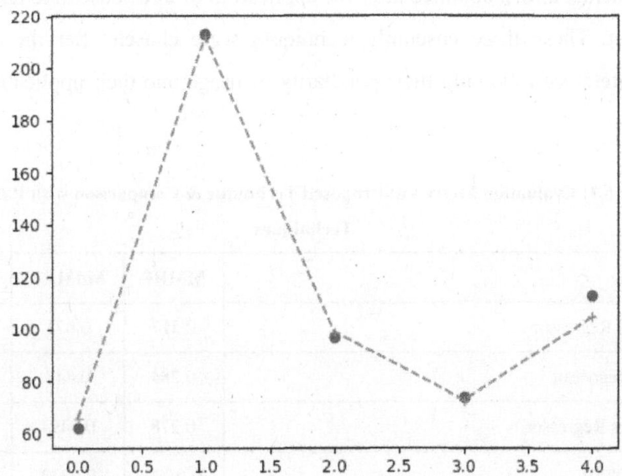

Figure 5.2: Predicted vs Observed Values (After Removing Bias and Fixing Slope

So after removing the bias value from it, we still can see that on a large trend if the graph gets extended more, the prediction error increases at each and every step, this is due to the inclined slope of our prediction, so to fix this we added another factor, that is, theta to the function, which works on fixing this error. So after neural network optimizing the value for these two factors, our prediction comes more accurate.

For slope, we have used equal spaced n values in range of 0.01 to 0.1, such that 0.01 is first value and 0.1 is last.

n - Number of values in input subset

Example -

If n =5, then the 4 slope values will be - 0.01, 0.25, 0.50. 0.75, 0.1

So these all are the attributes for neural network.

And the value of C (constant) is 25, all these values are optimally decided values received from backward propogation of neural network

The Table 5.1 shows the evaluation metrics of the proposed technique and proves that the proposed technique gives improved results in comparison with the earlier published techniques. Figures 5.3, 5.4 and 5.5 shows the plots for predicted effort vs. actual effort, obtained after the application of three ensemble techniques on the dataset. These three ensemble techniques were chosen after the analysis of existing literature following their popularity of usage and their applicability in this case.

Table 5.1: Evaluation Metrics of Proposed Technique & Comparison with Published Techniques

Algorithm	MMRE	MdMRE	Pred(8%)
Ada-Boost Regressor	0.317	0.671	20
Bagging Regressor	0.284	0.848	20
Extra Trees Regressor	0.278	0.0494	20
ABC_PSO[20]	0.0569	0.0333	NA
Zia [24]	0.0719	0.0714	57.14
SVC-NN Integrated Regressor (Proposed Method)	0.0353	0.0954	75

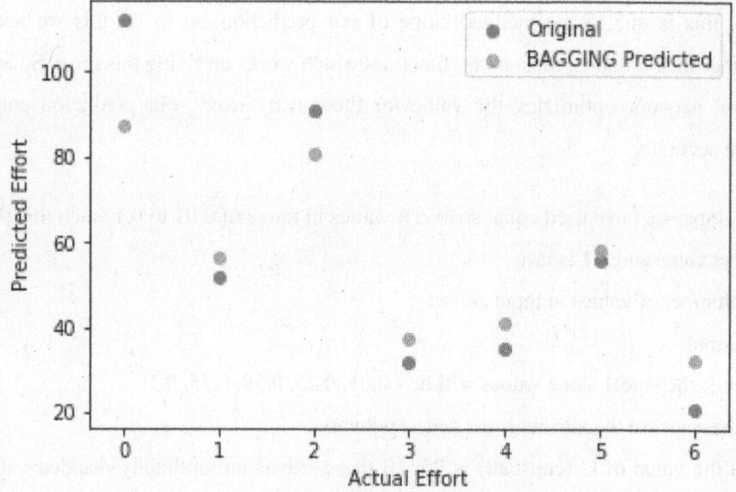

Figure 5.3: Bagging Predicted

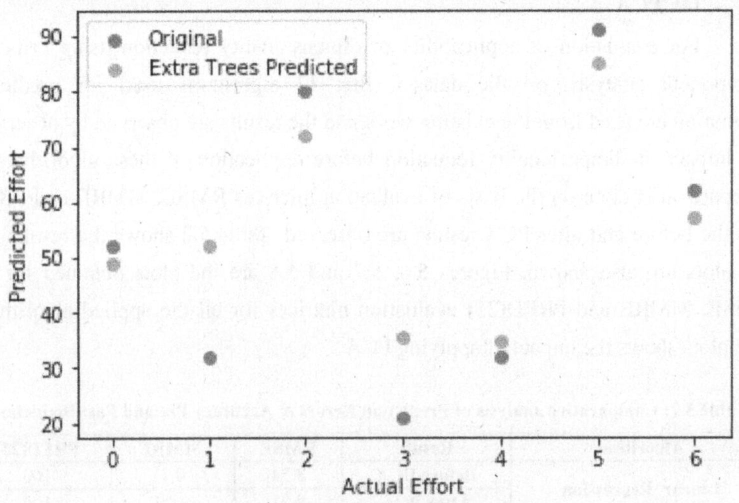

Figure 5.4: Extra Trees Predicted

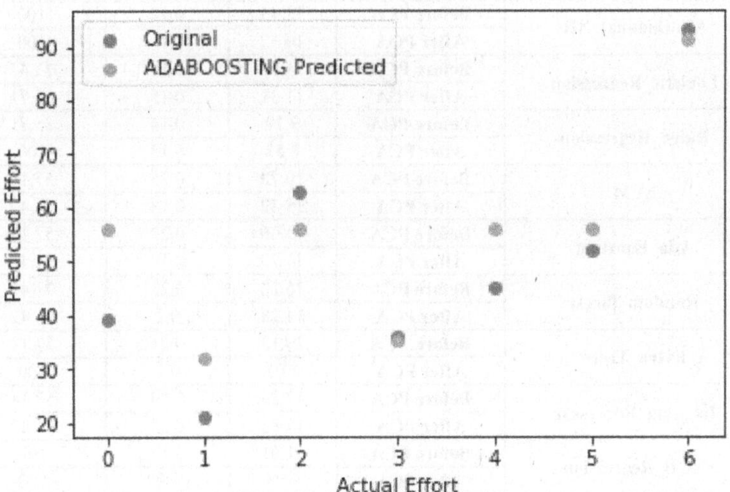

Figure 5.5: Adaboosting Predicted

5.2 RESULTS OBTAINED FOR EVALUATING THE APPLICABILITY OF PCA

For evaluation of applicability of dimensionality reduction using Principal Component analysis, on the dataset, first 12 algorithms used for predictive estimation are used from the existing work and the results are observed by observing the impact of dimensionality reduction before application of these algorithms. A comparison is done on the basis of evaluation metrices RMSE, MMRE and PRED and the before and after PCA results are observed. Table 5.2 shows the results and the plots are also shown. Figures 5.6, 5.7 and 5.8 are the plots obtained for the RMSE, MMRE and PRED(25) evaluation metrices for all the applied algorithms. The plots shows the impact of applying PCA

Table 5.2: Comparative analysis of Prediction Errors & Accuracy Pre and Post Reduction

Algorithm	Result	RMSE	MMRE	PRED(25)
Linear_Regression	Before PCA	8.54	0.1	100
	After PCA	8.21	0.09	100
Gaussian_NB	Before PCA	17.57	0.21	71.42
	After PCA	13.06	0.18	85.71
Bernoulli_NB	Before PCA	10.41	0.2	71.42
	After PCA	9.73	0.16	85.71
Multinomial_NB	Before PCA	12.43	0.12	100
	After PCA	10.52	0.11	100
Logistic_Regression	Before PCA	14.67	0.18	71.42
	After PCA	11.31	0.15	85.71
Ridge_Regression	Before PCA	9.79	0.14	85.71
	After PCA	8.57	0.13	100
SVM	Before PCA	16.78	0.25	57.14
	After PCA	15.32	0.18	71.42
Ada_Boosting	Before PCA	15.06	0.29	57.14
	After PCA	11.73	0.19	71.42
Random_forest	Before PCA	15.22	0.23	71.42
	After PCA	14.28	0.2	71.42
Extra_Trees	Before PCA	10.13	0.21	57.14
	After PCA	8.07	0.1	100
Bagging_Regressor	Before PCA	17.25	0.29	57.14
	After PCA	14.82	0.23	71.42
XGB_Regression	Before PCA	11.91	0.13	100
	After PCA	9.95	0.094	100

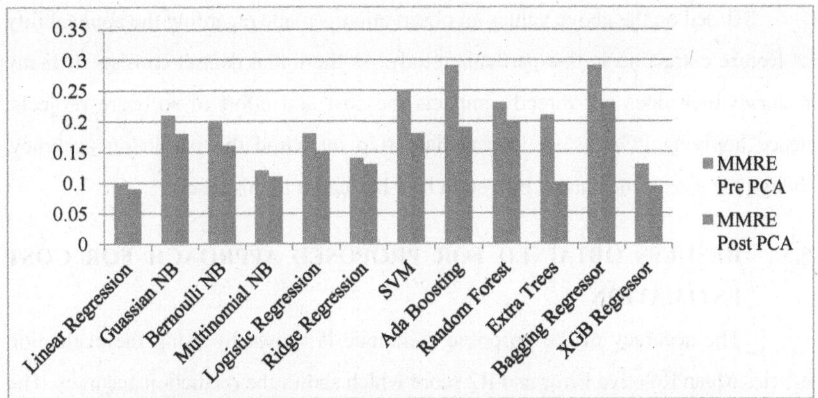

Figure 5.6: MMRE results for ensemble techniques pre PCA and post reduction

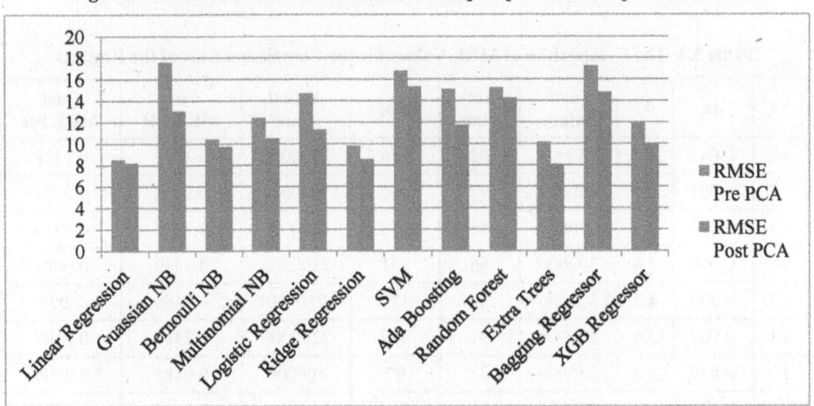

Figure 5.7: RMSE results for ensemble techniques pre and post reduction

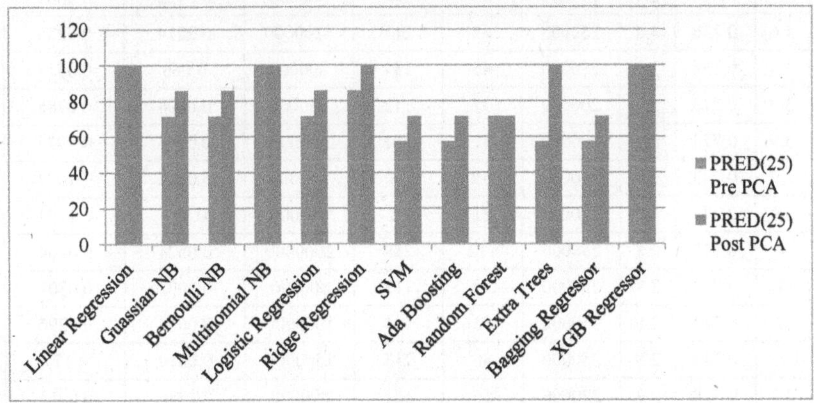

Figure 5.8: Prediction accuracy pre and post reduction

Based on the above values an observation is made regarding the applicability of feature extraction in this particular study. As the initial dataset consists of many factors which does not directly impacts the cost and effort of software projects, hence applying PCA as an intermediate step increased the prediction accuracy, though the size of the dataset proved to be a limitation in this case.

5.3 RESULTS OBTAINED FOR PROPOSED APPROACH FOR COST ESTIMATION

The accuracy of the proposed technique is shown by using the evaluation metrics Mean Relative Error and R2 score which shows the prediction accuracy. The results are shown in Table 5.3 & Table 5.4 respectively.

Table 5.3: The Comparison of MRE Values for the Completion Cost of the Projects

Vi	D	V	Team Salary	Act: Time	Effort	Actual Cost	Cost MRE LR	Cost MRE PR
4.2	0.687	2.7	230000	63	156	1200000	0.1166	0.1398
3.7	0.701	2.5	260000	92	202	1600000	0.1022	0.0091
4-	0.878	3.3	250000	56	173	1000000	0.1772	0.0519
4.5	0.886	3.8	300000	86	331	2100000	0.1349	0.0096
4.9	0.903	4.2	300000	32	124	750000	0.0466	0.023
4.1	0.903	3.6	400000	91	339	3200000	0.2347	0.0108
4.2	0.859	3.4	250000	35	97	600000	0.0185	0.0706
3.8	0.833	3	250000	93	257	1800000	0.0247	0.0376
3.9	0.646	2.4	190000	36	84	500000	0.0122	0.0685
4.6	0.758	3.2	250000	62	211	1200000	0.2214	0.0336
4.6	0.758	3.2	250000	45	131	800000	0.066	0.0513
3.9	0.773	2.9	200000	37	112	650000	0.0804	0.0785
3.9	0.773	2.9	200000	32	101	600000	0.0245	0.0973
3.9	0.773	2.9	200000	30	74	400000	0.0312	0.1677
3.9	0.773	2.9	200000	21	62	350000	0.107	0.1164
4	0.742	2.8	250000	112	289	2000000	0.0524	0.0404
4	0.742	2.8	250000	39	113	800000	0.1097	0.0309
4	0.742	2.8	250000	52	141	1000000	0.0645	0.0296
4	0.742	2.8	250000	80	213	1500000	0.0019	0.177
3.7	0.758	2.7	220000	56	137	800000	0.1386	0.0933
3.7	0.758	2.7	220000	35	91	550000	0.01	0.0914

Table 5.4: Comparison of Various Techniques for Cost Estimation of Projects

Technique	RMSE	R2_Score
Linear Regression	77087.31	0.95
Polynomial Regression	46933.66	0.98
Random Forest	48933.66	0.97

Based on these values various plots are obtained showing the prediction accuracy and the corresponding errors using Linear Regression, Polynomial Regression and Random Forest and it shows that the prediction accuracy is highest with least value of RMSE for the proposed Polynomial Regression. The prediction accuracy of the statistical model as proposed by (Ziauddin, 2012) was found to be 61.90, hence it is clearly observed that application of various machine learning techniques results in the increased prediction accuracy. The Figures 5.9, 5.10 and 5.11 shows the plots obtained after application of the mentioned three techniques for cost prediction.

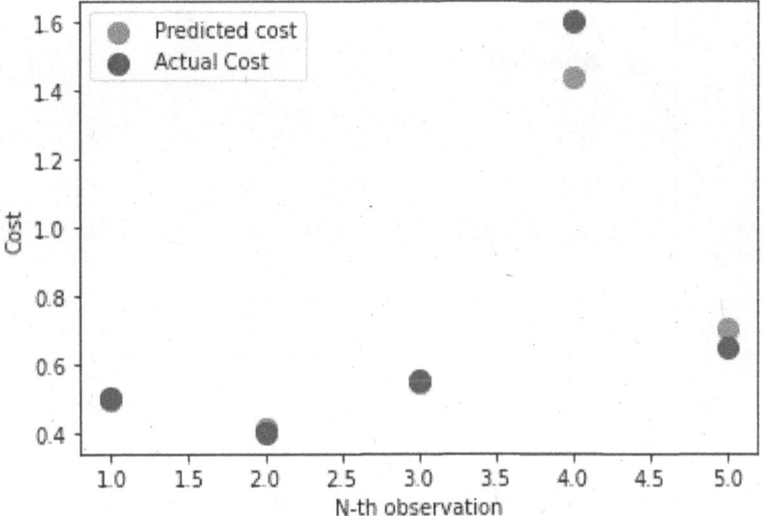

Figure 5.9: Cost Prediction using Linear Regression

85

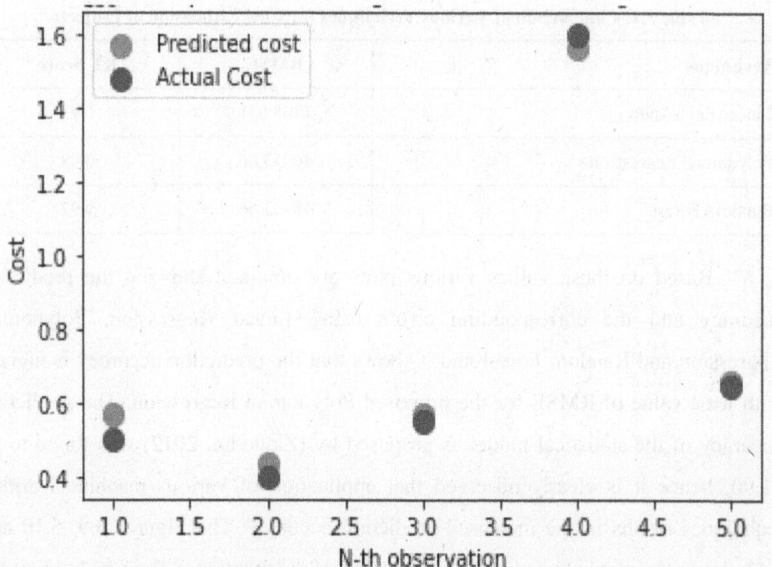

Figure 5.10: Cost Prediction Using Random Forest Regression

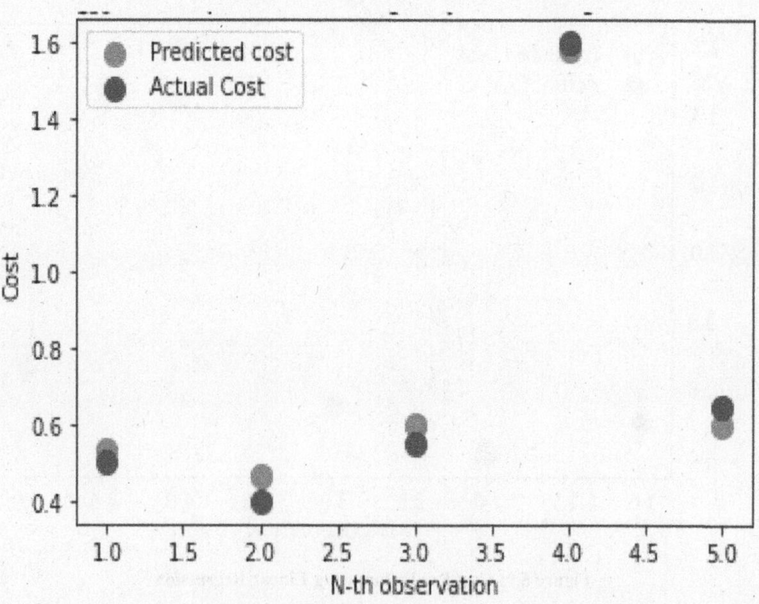

Figure 5.11: Cost Prediction Using Polynomial Regression

CHAPTER 6
CONCLUSION & CONTRIBUTION

Software estimation has been the research interest of many researchers criticism. The researchers indicate a disagreement that for projects developed using agile process, the accurate estimation is quiet difficult, as the requirements keep on changing throughout the development lifecycle and hence scope cannot be defined at early stage.. So, Customers' changing requirements and demand for unclear changes are the main reasons for the failure of estimation of practical measures for agile software projects.

This research work investigated non-algorithmic i.e. planning poker, algorithmic i.e. use case point and machine learning techniques for a comparative study. An extensive literature survey was conducted for related researches published in 2000-2022. The principal findings are summarized as follows:

- Machine Learning techniques give more accurate results as compared to non-Machine Learning models

- Different estimation techniques have different benefits and limitations. The identified and researched studies mentions that there are four major concerns in the estimation of agile projects: availability of small size of data sets, presence of outlier values, the features which are categorical and the missing values in the dataset.

- As there is no defined format for drafting of user stories, so the Estimation of projects using story point approach have some inhibitions.

- The ensemble techniques which are combination of individual techniques give better predication accuracy in comparison to the estimation by individual techniques.

CONTRIBUTION

In this work, we suggested a predictive model for estimating the effort of software projects specifically developed using agile. Using a dataset of 21 projects, we used an ensemble of SVR-RBF and ANN backpropogation which performed better in comparison with other ensemble based techniques. The results in terms of accuracy metrices MMRE, MAE and Pred(m) are studied and observed to deduce that two factors i.e. slope and bias have to be optimised for better accuracy of prediction of effort. The computations have been performed using Python Programming with SciKit library.

Though cost estimation has been a point of discussion amongst the researchers due to the negotiation practices prevailing now-a-days in softeare industry. Most of the reaercers claim that only effort shall be used as a practical measure for the prediction. Recently, th cost estimation has attracted a lot of attention of reseachers. In this work a simple regression model, a polynomial regression model and a random forest model was suggested for cost estimation of agile projects, and the results in terms of R2 score are shown for indicating the prediction error. The results showed that the polynomial regression gave better results for the used dataset as compared to other models as well as the statistical model proposed by (ZIauddin, 2017).

The work has proposed the significance of feature extraction in this case by using Principal Componenet Analysis. Using PCA the features having maximum weightage and impact on the target variable were retreived. The comparison tables and plots derived from the experimental evaluations showed that by applying PCA for extracting the features improved the performance of the algorithms, when measured using metrices MMRE, RMSE and Pred(25), irresepective of the algorithm. Significant results were obtained in reduction results irrespective of the small size of the available dataset.

SCOPE FOR FUTURE WORK

The future work targets the further optimization of the results and testing of the optimised results on other industrial datasets. The application of techniques like PCA and auto-encoders for the dimensions reduction and feature-weighting of the various features of dataset will further be used to check their impact on the prediction accuracy of effort. Further, other available ensemble technique may also be considered in the future work for optimizing the prediction acuuracy. One more issue that can be addressed in tuning of paramerters. Various optimization techniques like backpropogations and grid-search may be used.

REFERENCES

Abrahamsson, P. and Koskela, J. (2004) 'Extreme programming: A survey of empirical data from a controlled case study', in *Proceedings. 2004 International Symposium on Empirical Software Engineering, 2004.(ISESE'04)*, IEEE, pp. 73-82

Abrahamsson, P., Fronza, I., Moser, R., Vlasenko, J. and Pedrycz, W. (2011) 'Predicting development effort from user stories', in *2011 International Symposium on Empirical Software Engineering and Measurement*, IEEE, pp. 400-403..

Abrahamsson, P., Moser, R., Pedrycz, W., Sillitti, A. and Succi, G. (2007) 'Effort prediction in iterative software development processes--Incremental versus global prediction models', in *First International Symposium on Empirical Software Engineering and Measurement (ESEM 2007)*, IEEE, pp. 344-353.

Aljahdali, S., Sheta, A.F. and Debnath, N.C. (2015) 'Estimating software effort and function point using regression, Support Vector Machine and Artificial Neural Networks models' in *2015 IEEE/ACS 12th International Conference of Computer Systems and Applications (AICCSA)*, IEEE, pp. 1-8.

Amazal, F.A., Idri, A. and Abran, A. (2014) 'Software development effort estimation using classical and fuzzy analogy: a cross-validation comparative study', *International Journal of Computational Intelligence and Applications*, *13*(03), p.1450013.

Arora, M., Verma, S. and Chopra, S. (2020) 'A systematic literature review of machine learning estimation approaches in scrum projects', *Cognitive Informatics and Soft Computing*, pp.573-586.

Basri, S., Kama, N., Sarkan, H.M., Adli, S. and Haneem, F. (2016) 'An algorithmic-based change effort estimation model for software development', in *23rd Asia-Pacific Software Engineering Conference (APSEC)*, IEEE, pp. 177-184.

Beck, K., Beedle, M., Van Bennekum, A., Cockburn, A., Cunningham, W., Fowler, M., Grenning, J., Highsmith, J., Hunt, A., Jeffries, R. and Kern, J. (2001). The agile manifesto. http://www.ggilemanifesto.Org.

Benalal, T.R. and Mall, R. (2018) 'SEET: Software Development Effort Estimation Using Ensemble Techniques', *ACM SIGSOFT Software Engineering Notes*, 43(3), pp.17-21.

Britto, R., Mendes, E. and Börstler, J. (2015) 'An empirical investigation on effort estimation in agile global software development', in *2015 IEEE 10th international conference on global software engineering*, IEEE, pp.38-45.

Coelho, E. and Basu, A. (2012) 'Effort estimation in agile software development using story points', *International Journal of Applied Information Systems (IJAIS)*, 3(7).

Cohn, M. (2005) *Agile Estimating and Planning*. Prentice Hall PTR.

Cournapeau, D. (2018) *Scikit-learn: Machine learning in Python*—Scikit-learn 0.21. 2 documentation.

Cristal, M., Wildt, D. and Prikladnicki, R. (2008) 'Usage of Scrum practices within a global company', in *2008 IEEE International Conference on Global Software Engineering*, IEEE, pp. 222-226.

Documentation—XGBoost, X. (2020) *1.2. 0-SNAPSHOT documentation*. URL: https://xgboost. readthedocs. Io/en/latest/ (Accessed: 12/09/2019).

Dragicevic, S., Celar, S. and Turic, M. (2017) 'Bayesian network model for task effort estimation in agile software development', *Journal of systems and software*, 127, pp.109-119.

Gandomani, T.J., Wei, K.T. and Binhamid, A.K. (2014) 'A case study research on software cost estimation using experts' estimates, wideband Delphi and planning poker technique', *International Journal of Software Engineering and its Applications*, 8(11), pp. 173-182.

GARG, S. (2016)'*cost estimation model for agile software development projects using exploratory factor analysis and constraint programming approach factor analysis and constraint programming approach*' (thesis), DTU, Delhi.

Geurts, P. (2006). Ernst D. Wehenkel L. 'Extremely randomized trees. Machine Learning', 63(1), pp.3-42.

Grenning, J. (2002) 'Planning poker or how to avoid analysis paralysis while release planning', *Hawthorn Woods: Renaissance Software Consulting, 3*, pp.22-23.

Gultekin, M. and Kalipsiz, O. (2020). 'Story point-based effort estimation model with machine learning techniques', *International Journal of Software Engineering and Knowledge Engineering, 30*(01), pp.43-66.

Hameed, S., Elsheikh, Y. and Azzeh, M. (2022) 'An Optimized Case-Based Software Project Effort Estimation Using Genetic Algorithm', *Information and Software Technology*', p.107088.

Hamouda, A.E.D. (2014) 'Using agile story points as an estimation technique in cmmi organizations', *2014 agile conference*, IEEE, pp. 16-23.

Haugen, N.C. (2006) 'An empirical study of using planning poker for user story estimation', in *AGILE 2006 (AGILE'06,)* IEEE, pp. 9-13.

Hearty, P., Fenton, N., Marquez, D. and Neil, M. (2008) 'Predicting project velocity in xp using a learning dynamic bayesian network model', *IEEE Transactions on Software Engineering, 35*(1), pp.124-137.

Idri, A., Zakrani, A. and Zahi, A. (2010) 'Design of radial basis function neural networks for software effort estimation', *IJCSI International Journal of Computer Science Issues, 7*(4).

Jorgensen, M. (2007) 'Forecasting of software development work effort: Evidence on expert judgement and formal models', *International Journal of Forecasting, 23*(3), pp. 449-462.

Jørgensen, M. and Halkjelsvik, T. (2010) 'The effects of request formats on judgment-based effort estimation', *Journal of Systems and Software*, *83*(1), pp.29-36.

Jorgensen, M. and Shepperd, M. (2006) 'A systematic review of software development cost estimation studies', *IEEE Transactions on software engineering*, *33*(1), pp.33-53.

Khuat, T.T. and Le, M.H. (2016) 'An effort estimation approach for agile software development using fireworks algorithm optimized neural network', *Int J Comput Sci Inf Secur (IJCSIS)*, *14*(7), pp.122-130.

Khuat, T.T. and Le, M.H. (2018) 'A novel hybrid abc-pso algorithm for effort estimation of software projects using agile methodologies', *Journal of Intelligent Systems*, *27*(3), pp.489-506.

Kupiainen, E., Mäntylä, M.V. and Itkonen, J. (2015) 'Using metrics in Agile and Lean Software Development–A systematic literature review of industrial studies', *Information and software technology*, *62*, pp.143-163.

Li, Y.F., Xie, M. and Goh, T.N. (2009) 'A study of project selection and feature weighting for analogy based software cost estimation', *Journal of systems and software*, *82*(2), pp.241-252.

López-Martín, C. (2015) 'Predictive accuracy comparison between neural networks and statistical regression for development effort of software projects', *Applied Soft Computing*, *27*, pp.434-449.

Malgonde, O. and Chari, K. (2019) 'An ensemble-based model for predicting agile software development effort', *Empirical Software Engineering*, *24*(2), pp.1017-1055.

Malhotra, R., Kaur, A. and Singh, Y. (2010) 'Application of machine learning methods for software effort prediction', *ACM SIGSOFT Software Engineering Notes,* 35(3), pp.1-6.

Moeyersoms, J., de Fortuny, E.J., Dejaeger, K., Baesens, B. and Martens, D. (2015) 'Comprehensible software fault and effort prediction: A data mining approach', *Journal of Systems and Software, 100*, pp.80-90.

Molokken-Ostvold, K. and Haugen, N.C. (2007) 'Combining estimates with planning poker--an empirical study', in *2007 Australian Software Engineering Conference (ASWEC'07)*, IEEE, pp. 349-358.

Moløkken-Østvold, K., Jørgensen, M., Tanilkan, S.S., Gallis, H., Lien, A.C. and Hove, S.W. (2004) 'A survey on software estimation in the Norwegian industry', in *10th International Symposium on Software Metrics, 2004 Proceedings*, IEEE, pp. 208-219.

Moran, A. (2014). 'Agile risk management', *Agile Risk Management*, Springer, Cham, pp. 33-60.

Mustapha, H. and Abdelwahed, N. (2019) 'Investigating the use of random forest in software effort estimation. Procedia computer science', 148, pp.343-352.

Nassif, A.B., Azzeh, M., Capretz, L.F. and Ho, D. (2013) 'A comparison between decision trees and decision tree forest models for software development effort estimation', in *2013 Third International Conference on Communications and Information Technology (ICCIT)*, IEEE, pp. 220-224..

Nassif, A.B., Ho, D. and Capretz, L.F. (2013) 'Towards an early software estimation using log-linear regression and a multilayer perceptron model', *Journal of Systems and Software, 86*(1), pp.144-160.

Osman, H.H. and Musa, M.E. (2016) 'A survey of agile software estimation methods', *International journal of computer science and Telecommunications, 7*(3), pp.38-42.

Owais, M. and Ramakishore, R. (2016) 'Effort, duration and cost estimation in agile software development', *In 2016 Ninth International Conference on Contemporary Computing (IC3)*, IEEE, pp. 1-5.

Panda, A., Satapathy, S.M. and Rath, S.K. (2015) 'Empirical validation of neural network models for agile software effort estimation based on story points', *Procedia Computer Science, 57*, pp.772-781.

Pedregosa, F., Varoquaux, G., Gramfort, A., Michel, V., Thirion, B., Grisel, O., Blondel, M., Prettenhofer, P., Weiss, R., Dubourg, V. and Vanderplas, J. (2011) 'Scikit-learn: Machine learning in Python', *the Journal of machine Learning research, 12*, pp.2825-2830.

Perkusich, M., e Silva, L.C., Costa, A., Ramos, F., Saraiva, R., Freire, A., Dilorenzo, E., Dantas, E., Santos, D., Gorgônio, K. and Almeida, H. (2020) 'Intelligent software engineering in the context of agile software development: A systematic literature review', *Information and Software Technology*, 119, p.106241.

Power, K. (2011) 'Using silent grouping to size user stories', *International Conference on Agile Software Development*, Springer, Berlin, Heidelberg, pp. 60-72.

Prasada Rao, C., Siva Kumar, P., Rama Sree, S. and Devi, J. (2018) 'An agile effort estimation based on story points using machine learning techniques', in *Proceedings of the Second International Conference on Computational Intelligence and Informatics* Springer, Singapore pp. 209-219.

Santana, C., Leoneo, F., Vasconcelos, A. and Gusmão, C. (2011) 'Using function points in agile projects', in *International Conference on Agile Software Development*, Springer, Berlin, Heidelberg, pp. 176-191.

Satapathy, S.M. and Rath, S.K. (2014) 'Class point approach for software effort estimation using various support vector regression kernel methods', *Proceedings of the 7th India Software Engineering Conference* pp. 1-10

Satapathy, S.M. and Rath, S.K. (2017) 'Empirical assessment of machine learning models for agile software development effort estimation using story points', *Innovations in Systems and Software Engineering, 13*(2), pp.191-200.

Satapathy, S.M., Acharya, B.P. and Rath, S.K. (2014) 'Class point approach for software effort estimation using stochastic gradient boosting technique', *ACM SIGSOFT Software Engineering Notes*, *39*(3), pp.1-6.

Satapathy, S.M., Acharya, B.P. and Rath, S.K. (2016) 'Early stage software effort estimation using random forest technique based on use case points'. *IET Software*, 10(1), pp.10-17.

Sehra, S.K., Brar, Y.S., Kaur, N. and Sehra, S.S. (2017) 'Research patterns and trends in software effort estimation', *Information and Software Technology*, *91*, pp.1-21.

Sharma, P. and Singh, J. (2017) 'Systematic literature review on software effort estimation using machine learning approaches', in 2017 International Conference on Next Generation Computing and Information Systems (ICNGCIS), IEEE (pp. 43-47).

Shinji, K. and Schigeo, H. (2004) 'Estimating Effort by Use Case Points: Method, Tool and Case Study', in *Proceedings of the 10th International Symposium on Software Metrics (METRICS'04)* pp. 1430-1435

Singh, M. (2008) 'U-SCRUM: An agile methodology for promoting usability', in *Agile 2008 Conference*, IEEE, pp. 555-560.

Tanveer, B., Guzmán, L. and Engel, U.M. (2016) 'Understanding and improving effort estimation in agile software development: An industrial case study', in *Proceedings of the international conference on software and systems process.* pp. 41-50.

Trendowicz, A. and Jeffery, R. (2014) 'Software project effort estimation', *Foundations and Best Practice Guidelines for Success, Constructive Cost Model–COCOMO*, pp.277-293.

Ungan, E., Cizmeli, N. and Demirörs, O. (2014) 'Comparison of functional size based estimation and story points, based on effort estimation effectiveness in

SCRUM projects', in *2014 40th EUROMICRO Conference on Software Engineering and Advanced Applications,* IEEE pp. 77-80.

Usman, M., Mendes, E., Weidt, F. and Britto, R. (2014) 'Effort estimation in agile software development: a systematic literature review', in *Proceedings of the 10th international conference on predictive models in software engineering.* pp 82-91.

Vyas, M., Bohra, A., Lamba, C.S. and Vyas, A. (2018) 'A review on software cost and effort estimation techniques for agile development process', *Int J Recent Res Aspects,* 5(1), pp.1-5.

Weflen, E., Korniejczuk, K., Lau, S., Kryk, S., MacKenzie, C.A. and Rivero, I.V. (2018) 'Application of Bayesian Belief Network for Agile Kanban Backlog Estimation', in *Proceedings of the 2018 IISE Annual Conference.*

Wen, J., Li, S., Lin, Z., Hu, Y. and Huang, C. (2012) 'Systematic literature review of machine learning based software development effort estimation models', *Information and Software Technology,* 54(1), pp.41-59.

Zakrani, A., Najm, A. and Marzak, A. (2018) 'Support vector regression based on grid-search method for agile software effort prediction', *2018 IEEE 5th International Congress on Information Science and Technology (CiSt),* IEEE pp. 1-6.

Ziauddin, K.Z.K., Tipu, S.K. and Zia, S. (2012) 'An Intelligent Software Effort Estimation System', *Journal of Expert Systems (JES),* 1(4), pp.91-98.

Milton Keynes UK
Ingram Content Group UK Ltd.
UKHW041043120923
428519UK00001B/19

9 781916 706910